To Gary

It was a real Honor
to serve with your
          Brother

God Bless America

          Curtis P Gay

ONE MORE SUNRISE

Memoir of a Combat Infantryman in Viet Nam

CURTIS P. GAY

This is how we know what love is: Jesus Christ laid down his life for us. And we ought to lay down our lives for our brothers and sisters.

1 John 3:16

authorHOUSE®

AuthorHouse™
1663 Liberty Drive
Bloomington, IN 47403
www.authorhouse.com
Phone: 1-800-839-8640

First published by AuthorHouse 3/16/2011

ISBN: 978-1-4567-5440-2 (e)
ISBN: 978-1-4567-5441-9 (hc)
ISBN: 978-1-4567-5442-6 (sc)

Library of Congress Control Number: 2011904366

Printed in the United States of America

MY PERSONAL MISSION

America's homeless veterans have served in World War II, the Korean War, Cold War, Vietnam War, Grenada, Panama, Lebanon, Afghanistan and Iraq (OEF/OIF), and the military's anti-drug cultivation efforts in South America. Nearly half of homeless veterans served during the Vietnam era. Two-thirds served our country for at least three years, and one-third were stationed in a war zone.

About 1.5 million other veterans, meanwhile, are considered at risk of homelessness due to poverty, lack of support networks, and dismal living conditions in overcrowded or substandard housing.

Although flawless counts are impossible to come by – the transient nature of homeless populations presents a major difficulty – VA estimates that **107,000** veterans are homeless on any given night. Over the course of a year, approximately twice that many experience homelessness. Only eight percent of the general population can claim veteran status, but nearly one-fifth of the homeless population are veterans.

The most effective programs for homeless and at-risk veterans are community-based, nonprofit, "veterans helping veterans" groups. Programs that seem to work best feature transitional housing with the camaraderie of living in structured, substance-free environments with fellow veterans who are succeeding at bettering themselves.

Government money, while important, is currently limited, and available services are often at capacity. It is critical, therefore, that community groups reach out to help provide the support, resources and opportunities most Americans take for granted: housing, employment and health care. Veterans who participate in collaborative programs are afforded more services and have higher chances of becoming tax-paying, productive citizens again

To this end, proceeds from the sale of this book will be used to assist homeless veterans.

Thank you

ACKNOWLEDGMENTS

My daughters, Dawn, Kristi, and Angi have encouraged me to write this book for years---so here it is girls—I Love You!

My wife Susan has tolerated me much longer than most women would. I Love You too, Susan. Susan and my great friend Judy Alford edited this work for me. Thanks, ladies.

Special thanks to Baz Cunningham, author of <u>Three-Stone Fires- A Novel of Haiti in 1982</u> and Frank Evans, author of <u>STAND TO----A Journey to Manhood</u> for their advice and encouragement throughout the process of putting this book together. Credit Frank Gabelman for the picture of A Company on patrol on the cover of this book.

My Cacti Comrades-In-Arms---Art Johnson, Dave Dunn, Frank Gabelman, John Pearman, Mike Riley, Roger Bolerjack, Steve Putnam, and Tom Gardner—who encouraged me, reminded me, corrected me, and furnished pictures—thank you for being there for me both now and back when.

Thank you, Dear Readers, for allowing me to share my story with you.

And thanks be to God for allowing me to enjoy so many sunrises!

CONTENTS

INTRODUCTION

Most of you don't know me. But I'm sure you know somebody just like me. I could be your father or grandfather. Maybe I'm somebody you work with or for. You'll find me teaching at universities and living under bridges. We kneel beside you at church and haul away your trash on Thursday.

About two and a half million Americans served in the Viet Nam War. One out of ten Americans who served in Viet Nam was a casualty. 58,148 were killed and 304,000 more were wounded. The average infantryman in the South Pacific during World Was II saw about 40 days of combat in four years. The average infantryman in Viet Nam saw about 240 days of combat in one year. Why have you never heard about all this? Because we don't talk about it.

There is nothing glorious about being involved in the death of another human being. Everybody in Viet Nam was in danger at all times. These are difficult subjects to share with anybody who wasn't there---especially loved ones. So we didn't talk about it with our mothers, sisters, and wives.

The main veteran's organizations of the era were the American Legion and the Veterans of Foreign Wars. These groups were mostly populated and run by World War II veterans. The general consensus among those guys was that we weren't in a real war. It felt as if we could join but we could never really belong. So we couldn't talk to them about our experiences either.

Viet Nam was a very controversial and divisive war. Antiwar demonstrations were commonplace. Unfortunately, a lot of the protesters wrongly placed the blame on the individual soldiers. Even more unfortunate, a lot of the protesters were family and friends. So we couldn't talk to them about it.

If this wasn't enough, the media enjoyed circulating rumors that we were all crazy drug addicts. We weren't, but that was the stereotype that existed. As a result, most of us just didn't identify ourselves as Viet Nam veterans. When found out, we just said we didn't want to talk about it. So we didn't. Still don't.

We all like to believe that if we ignore something long enough it will go away. This is something that won't go away by itself. These deep feelings just fester and rot away at our self respect and worth. Many of us have had chemical dependency, relationship, and employment problems as a direct result of these suppressed emotions which we have kept pent up inside for decades. Writing this book has been great therapy for me. If I can encourage just one other veteran to tell his story then it was worth every bit of effort.

Please keep in mind that this is a memoir. According to the Oxford Companion to Military History a memoir is "An account of historical events as viewed by a participant or contemporary. These take various forms, depending upon the events being described, the rank and perspective of the writer, and the motives for the production of such an account. Military memoirs may be divided, broadly, into two categories: those produced by politicians and generals, offering an insight into key decisions and a top-down view of the events; and those of the officers and men who witnessed the front-line action—" These are my memories of what happened to me.

Two people can stand next to each other and have totally different recollections of the same event. Allow 45 years to pass while trying to suppress these memories and the viewpoints really differ. Did I get some things wrong? Probably. I have made every effort to be as accurate as I can while keeping this memoir exactly what it is-----"An account of historical events by a participant----the officers and men who witnessed the front-line action". My only motive is to help you, the reader, get a feeling for what being a combat infantryman in Viet Nam was like.

For those of you with no military experience, I have included a glossary and charts describing Army units and ranks. These are at the back of they book. I hope they are helpful.

Thank you for letting me share my story with you.

ONE MORE SUNRISE

No one actually sees a sunrise in the jungle. You sense it and you feel it. It is more of an experience than an event. But you don't see it with your eyes. The darkness slowly changes to daylight. This is what I live for--- one more sunrise.

I unwrap myself from my dingy poncho liner. The nights are warm enough that I really don't need a blanket, but it keeps the mosquitoes off me. Slowly I arise from the shallow pit I dug last night for a foxhole, holding my rifle in my hand. My rifle has become a part of me by now, an extension of my body just like my foot or my arm.

Over to my left I hear Rodebaugh moving around. His thick New Jersey accent makes me think he's swearing even when he's just talking. He's talking to Waycaster, the guy from West Virginia he shared a foxhole with last night.

To my right are Howard and Hernandez. "Happy" Howard is from the projects of Detroit and William Hernandez is from Puerto Rico. Out here we have no black or white, only olive drab, the color of our uniforms.

Rawhide and Cabby, the machine gun crew, occupy the next hole. Rawhide worked on a cattle ranch in Montana before being drafted; Cabby drove a taxi in Detroit. Together we are called the "Third Herd". Officially we are the Third Squad, Third Platoon. A Company, Second Battalion, Thirty-fifth Infantry Regiment, Third Brigade Task Force, Twenty-Fifth Infantry Division.

The squad is getting busy with morning chores. The routine is pretty much the same for the other three squads in the platoon and the other three platoons in the Company. A meal of canned food is washed down with some instant coffee. Then comes the repacking of gear and refilling of foxholes. Not long after sunrise, the order to "saddle-up" will be given and we will be on the march again. Where to? Most of us don't know where we are to begin with; let alone where we are going. We know we are somewhere in Viet Nam, and that's about it. We're pretty sure the officers know where we are and where we're going. At least we hope they do. After another day of struggling through the jungle in the heat and humidity we will stop again just before dark, dig in, and do it all over again. That is, unless we meet the enemy. Then things change. Fast.

Rodebaugh is carrying on about a new sports contest which will take place this week back in the States. The 1967 Super Bowl is what they are calling it. If it proves successful it may turn into an annual event. Rodebaugh can't believe that the team from the young American Football League thinks they can begin to compete with Vince Lombardi and the Green Bay Packers. Why, seven years ago these Kansas City Chiefs didn't even exist! Waycaster doesn't really care about football or any other sport. He just listens and comments often enough to keep Rodebaugh fired up. You would swear they were a married couple the way they carry on.

While the guys are getting their gear together I need to go find the Platoon Sergeant and get our orders for the day. Me? Oh yeah. I almost forgot to tell you who I am. I'm Sergeant Curt Gay, Squad Leader of the Third Herd. That sounds strange and in a way sad to me. Six months ago Rodebaugh, Waycaster, Hernandez, and I were just four green replacements to a seasoned A Company. Being the new guys had bonded us together. We're still tight, but since I made Sergeant there is a distance between us like a wedge. I have to give the orders and they have to follow them. Sometimes they feel like they have to remind me of those days. I really haven't forgotten. How could I?

Sergeant Curt Gay

Heat like I had never felt before rocked me backwards when I stepped from the plane onto the airstrip six months ago. My uniform was instantly drenched with sweat. The air was not only hot-it was heavy with moisture. It wrapped itself around me like it wanted to drag me down and melt me on the spot. Just a month ago I was hunkered down in the snow in Germany trying to keep warm. How was I going to take a whole year of this heat? I grabbed my duffle bag out of the huge pile of identical bags and joined the other new replacements on the blazing tarmac.

A squad of MPs was soon standing around the group.

"Men, I know that some of you are carrying contraband", said the Sergeant as he strolled back and forth in front of the group. "We are here to offer you one and only one chance to get rid of anything you have brought that is illegal. So get in your bags and put that kind of stuff on the ground. Nobody will be punished. No questions will be asked. So take out your switch-blade knifes, unauthorized guns, liquor, drugs, whatever. You will be searched before being assigned to your units. So get rid of it now and save us all a lot of trouble down the road."

A mad shuffle followed. I worried about the Western Bowie knife I had in my bag, but decided to take a chance and keep it. When we marched away the field was littered with bottles and weapons. Nobody was ever searched. I have often wondered how much of the so- called contraband became the personal property of the MPs.

With little ceremony we were moved to the replacement center for processing. A small colony of squad tents became my home for the next few days. Each tent housed twenty soldiers. Folding metal cots with thin mattresses served as beds. The sides of the tents were made of mosquito netting. Canvas panels could be let down for more protection and privacy but these stayed rolled up and tied most of the time. Sometimes we were sent on work details but most of the time was spent sitting around sharing our stories.

It was a time of great excitement and anticipation. Most of us really had no idea what we were in for. We were almost giddy about the great adventure we were on, almost like school kids on the way to a picnic. Some guys had personal weapons they had brought from home. One young Sergeant wore a chrome plated, long barreled revolver around camp in a hand-tooled western style holster. Another had a steelhead tomahawk slung on his side from a beaded belt. I just had to ask these warriors where they were assigned. Quick Draw was a cook. Tomahawk Man was a mechanic. So much for first impressions.

All our money was exchanged for something called Military Pay Currency. These funny looking pieces of paper would be the only currency, aside from Vietnamese money, that we would see for the next year. It was explained to us that American greenbacks were a hot item on the local black market.

The only detail I got assigned to at this replacement center was the trash run. The truck was fully loaded with trash before I was picked up. The Specialist driving the truck had me climb in the passenger side of the cab and we were off. He must have known the road by memory since it was raining so hard visibility was reduced to only a few feet ahead. The wipers couldn't keep up with the rain. We soon arrived in front of the largest steel building I had ever seen.

"This is the office" announced the Specialist. "Go on inside. I'll dump this load and come back for you. Make yourself comfortable, we're going to be here for awhile."

I jumped out and dodged raindrops all the way to the door. After taking two steps inside, I just stopped and stared in amazement. I had never seen anything like it! Hundreds of soldiers stood around in clusters talking. Along the walls were vendors of everything from beer to jewelry. At the far end of the building was an office of some kind, but the rest resembled an indoor bazaar. I bought a cold beer and joined a group of guys I recognized from camp. Every so often a very young looking Vietnamese girl would emerge from a side room, grab another guy, and disappear back into the room. Traders were circulating the room peddling everything from medals to marijuana. For a young country boy, all this was overwhelming. I watched all this foreign activity for two hours before the Specialist decided it was time to head back. That had to be the best work detail I had ever been assigned to!

WELCOME TO PLEIKU

After spending a few days in the replacement center a group of us were loaded on a convoy of trucks. We traveled the muddy Highway 14 north to a place called Dragon Mountain Base Camp near Pleiku. It was the beginning of the monsoon season and it rained every day. The red clay that had been dust just months before became a gooey, sticky mess that clung to everything.

As we approached the base camp we saw a small squad of men on patrol. The Sergeant was much larger than the rest. He chewed on a cigar as he eyed the convoy of trucks. Following him closely was another soldier carrying a radio. The antenna swayed back and forth in rhythm with his stride. The other men seemed so vigilant that they could explode at any minute. I was taken with how tough and calloused these men appeared to be. These were obviously the hardened veterans one rarely sees except on the very front lines. I had no idea that I was looking at the original Third Herd.

The replacement depot at Pleiku was very similar to the one I had just left, only smaller. During processing a clerk looked up in surprise.

"PFC Gay, you enlisted to be a clerk-typist. How in the world did you end up in the Infantry?"

I grinned as I remembered myself and the other newly graduated basic trainees clustered around the Company bulletin board to see where we were going for advanced training. After the crowd thinned I took a look. Most of the others didn't know where they would be assigned. They were either drafted or had open enlistments. I had a guarantee from my Recruiter-in writing!-that I would have a nice, soft career as a Company Clerk. What a surprise it was to see that I was going to Fort Polk, Louisiana! Beside my name was the notation "MOS 11B". I knew what MOS stood for-Military Occupation Specialty. I had no idea what 11B was.

"Drill Sergeant, I didn't know they have a Clerk-Typist School at Fort Polk."

With a great belly laugh, the Drill Sergeant broke my heart. "They don't, son. All they train at Fort Polk is Infantry.11B, huh? That's Light Weapons Infantry. If you can pick up a weapon and carry it you'll be trained to shoot it. Yer gonna be a grunt, sonny."

"But I have a guaranteed enlistment to be a clerk-typist!"

"You didn't read the fine print, lad. If your school of choice is full, they can put you anywhere they want. And they want to put you in the Infantry."

I quickly came back to the present when I heard the clerk say,"We're short on clerks here in Headquarters Company. We'll put you in on-the-job training and keep you here. They never should have sent you to the Infantry to begin with. "

Happy with the reassignment, I was soon in a tent in Headquarters Company with three other clerks.

Before beginning any duties I had to attend a week-long orientation program. We learned a lot of stuff that was specific to Viet Nam--- booby traps, pungi stakes, taking a pill daily to prevent catching malaria, and the tricky business of moving through the jungle. We soon learned that jungle travel was not a walk in the park. Being a clerk was really sounding good to me now. I received my Combat Infantryman's Badge--- an award given only to infantrymen who had met enemy fire---- when our night patrol training team was fired on. One shot, fired from an undeterminable location and hitting nobody, rang out of the darkness. The young Lieutenant following me in the column beamed broadly.

"Can you believe it? One week in Viet Nam and I've earned my CIB!"

Neither of us fully understood at the time what it meant to actually EARN the award!

I had become friends with another clerk in training named Haymaker. He had also enlisted as a clerk-typist and found himself trained as a tank crew member. Haymaker hated the idea that he wasn't going to see combat.

"How am I going to explain to my grandchildren that I went off to war and all I did was punch on a typewriter?"

On the next to last day of orientation an Infantry Major came around to observe how things were going. During a break, Haymaker and I approached the Major.

Haymaker spoke first.

"Sir, may we have a moment of your time?"

"Certainly, soldier, what's on your mind?"

"Well, Sir, I am a trained tanker and this man is a Light Weapons Infantryman. We have been assigned as OJT clerks but I really would rather be out in the field."

"Well!!---We have all the tankers we need." Then he said with a large grin,"But we need all the infantry we can get---- 11B, huh?"

After the last day of orientation I found myself assigned to A Company, 2nd Battalion of the 35th Infantry Regiment, 3rd Brigade Task Force, of the 25th Infantry Division. I soon discovered that in the last month A Company had lost most of its Sergeants and their Company Commander during some very intense fighting. Ironically enough, I was in the Third Squad, the same bedraggled squad I had seen on patrol the day I arrived in Pleiku.

I finally got equipped with the proper gear. The Supply Sergeant issued me new jungle boots, web gear and a pack, and a poncho with a poncho liner. I was also issued an M-16 rifle. It was the first M-16 I had ever seen up close. Having been trained with the much heavier M-14 rifle, I thought the shorter, lighter M-16 would be much easier to carry through the jungle. It was sort of strange looking, though. The hard plastic pistol-grip stock didn't seem nearly as sturdy as the wooden stock of the M-14. The plastic forehand grip that wrapped around the barrel reminded me of the futuristic toy guns we played with when we were kids.

"It's swell, it's by Mattel©" joked the supply clerk as he handed me my weapon and ammunition magazines.

It did look like some kind of toy compared to any other rifle I had ever seen. I had no idea how bonded I would become to that little rifle we found so funny at the time.

The jungle fatigue uniforms I was issued were much lighter than the uniforms I was accustomed to wearing. The shirt didn't tuck in; it was more like a jacket with four pockets. I now had pockets everywhere, even on my legs. The uniforms were comfortable but obviously used. The unfaded areas on the sleeves and the name on the nametag indicated that the uniforms once belonged to a Sergeant named Hopkins.

"I won't get in trouble with Sergeant Hopkins for wearing his uniforms, will I?"

The supply clerk never even looked up from his work.

"Don't worry. He won't need them anymore."

I exchanged Hopkins' uniforms the next uniform day. By then I had my own uniforms with my own name on them.

I don't think an Infantryman ever masters the art of organizing and adjusting his equipment. That may sound strange, since there really isn't much equipment involved. It all starts with the pistol belt. This is a wide, thick belt made of canvas. The metal grommet holes that are evenly spaced along its length serve as attachment points for any issued equipment. The length of the belt needs to be adjusted so it rides below your regular belt to avoid pinching but not too long so it slides off your hips when you walk. Simple enough until you add equipment or the belt gets wet, causing the belt to stretch. Then, all the attached equipment has to be removed before the belt can be readjusted.

A small pack attaches to the belt and is centered in the back. Two straps on the bottom of the pack allow the attachment of a rolled up poncho and poncho liner. If nothing is placed in the pack, the belt is enough support for it. Since it is unlikely that somebody living in the jungle would ever have an empty pack, the shoulder harness is needed for support. Much like a pair of suspenders, the shoulder harness attaches to the top of the pack in the back and to the pistol belt in the front. Most guys attached a grenade or their first aid pouch on the shoulder of the harness opposite their shooting arm. I carried my bowie knife taped upside down on my harness with camouflage duct tape.

The Company I was now a part of had just come back from Operation Paul Revere. They had been in the field a long time and had seen a lot of action. They were in base camp at Pleiku to rest up and get replacements. Not only had they lost a lot of men, some of them were completing their time in the service. Although there was a lot of busy work going on, most of their time was spent resting up or conducting short patrols that didn't draw any action.

"You fresh meat, come with me!"

Four of us, A Companies latest replacements, had been inside the squad tent just long enough to figure out which bunks were occupied and which could be ours when the Sergeant appeared in the doorway. His boots clomped on the rough-sawn plank floor as he paced back and forth between us. His deeply tanned face wrinkled up like he smelled something distasteful as he looked us over. His blank, expressionless eyes seemed to look all the way through us.

"C'mon, party time is over."

We waited for the formal commands we were used to, such as "Fall In" or "Attention" or "Column of Twos". Realizing that wasn't going to happen, we followed the Sergeant out of the tent into the blistering heat. Our clothing was instantly drenched with sweat, almost as if our skin was leaking.

A leisurely stroll of about a hundred yards brought us to the perimeter of the base camp beside a guard tower. The soldier in the tower glanced down at us briefly before returning to reading his mail from home.

We stopped in front of a fence of concertina wire. This stuff reminded me of a large Slinky Toy© made of barbed wire. It was stretched out and staked down to make an obstacle for the enemy to try to get through if they attacked. This fence had rolls of wire stacked three high.

Between us and the triple row of concertina wire was a pile of burlap bags and a couple of shovels. On the other side of the concertina wire the landscape had been stripped bare for 500 yards or so.

"Captain wants these sandbags filled and double stacked all the way between this tower and the next. I'll be back."

With that, the Sergeant spun on his heel and stormed off like a man who had just taken out the garbage.

"Welcome to the Nam," chuckled the man in the tower.

"Reckon we had best git to it," declared Waycaster.

He walked slightly slumped over anyway, so his long, lanky arm just seemed to scoop up the nearest shovel.

"These hyar bags ain't agonna fill theyselves."

Rodebaugh picked up one of the sandbags and held it for Waycaster to fill. Hernandez and I teamed up filling the other pile of sandbags.

Waycaster never seemed to cease talking, even as sweat dripped like a leaky faucet from the odd little mole on the right side of his nose.

"We shore wuddn't be doin nuthin like this if we wuz back home in Tyler County. Nosuh. Rat about now we'd be asittin undah a shade tree sippin a little white likker."

"Where the hell is Tyler County?" groused Rodebaugh.

"West By God Virginia. You talk kinder funny. Where you from anyway? I kin tell yer some kinder Yankee."

"Paterson, New Jersey, Muthefukka. You wanna make sumpin of it?"

The bantering went back and forth as Hernandez held bags for me to fill.

His smiling dark face let me know that he realized, as I did, that our fellow squad members were only playing, sort of feeling each other out.

We had been filling sandbags for about an hour when Rodebush said "What the hell is that stink?"

Looking back towards the camp, we saw two soldiers wearing bandanas across their faces stirring 55 gallon drums that had been cut in half. Gigantic columns of black smoke boiled out of the drums and drifted towards us. The stench was almost unbearable. It not only filled our nostrils but even seemed to penetrate our pores.

The soldier in the tower looked up from his mail.

"You guys think you got it bad? Those guys have to burn the shithouse. They must have really pissed somebody off!"

"What the hell are they doing?" demanded Rodebush.

"Those cans sit under the holes in the latrine. When they get full, somebody has to drag them out, pour gasoline in them, set it on fire, and stir it until it's all burnt up."

"Damn!" said Waycaster. "Gimme another sandbag. All of a sudden this detail got to lookin' a whole lot better."

The sun was straight up in the sky when we saw the Sergeant returning. He stopped about fifty feet away, yelled "Chow", spun on his heel, and was gone again. We all looked at each other, wondering what to do next. All of us were so conditioned to being put into some kind of formation and marched wherever we went that the idea of just going somewhere without a bunch of hoopla was still totally foreign to us.

"Reckin it's time fer lunch", declared Waycaster.

He threw down his shovel and began strolling towards the Company area with the rest of us close behind. We found the mess hall and went in. We picked up trays, went through the line, sat down and ate, all with nobody giving us direction. Formality in our military lives was officially over.

The next morning, the Supply Sergeant poked his head in the tent. After looking us over he made his request.

"Any of you guys know how to paint?"

This was a strange question since all our structures were tents. My Grandfather and Uncle were in the painting and paper hanging business and I had helped them a few times in the summer. I had been mostly assigned to scraping and cleaning up, but nobody had to know that.

"I'm a painter."

"Come with me".

We went down to the far end of the Company area and entered a tent which was obviously used for storage.

In the middle of the tent sat a very faded Company sign surrounded by an assortment or artists brushes and oil paints.

"There you go, have at it!"

Obviously, there had been a mistake.

"Sarge, I'm not that kind of painter!"

"What the Hell kinda painter are you then?'" he declared, eyeing me suspiciously.

It occurred to me that all I had to do was paint over the existing art and lettering, none of which was very intricate. It also occurred to me that I would be inside, out of the glaring sun, until I finished the project.

"Never mind," I recanted. "I'll get right on it."

I began by taking a quick inventory of my supplies. Then I placed the sign on a table to give it a good cleaning. As I scrubbed, I tried in vain to understand what the emblem had to do with the Infantry. It really made no sense to me.

Crest of Second Battalion Thirty-Fifth Infantry Regiment

The large white shield had a big cactus plant in the center. A blue square occupied the upper left corner. The edges of the square were perforated much like a postage stamp. A white Maltese cross was in the center of the blue square. In the center of the cross was a red acorn.

I had all my brushes and paint ready to use when the Supply Sergeant returned.

"You have everything you need?"

"Almost, Sarge. I'm going to need some green paint for this cactus. It's so faded it looks like it's blue."

"It's supposed to be blue."

"What? A blue cactus?"

Okay. I didn't understand this crest before and now I'm really confused.

"Why a blue cactus?"

The Sergeant walked over to an old cot in the corner of the tent and sat down. He lit up a cigarette and began to educate me.

"I can help you with all that. You see, I'm sort of a history nut. The 35th Infantry Regiment was formed in 1916 in Arizona to provide security along the Mexican border. Pancho Villa had been raiding towns along the border.. That's where the cactus plant comes from. It represents the desert country around Nogales.

Three smaller units were put together to form the 35th. They were the 11th Infantry, the 18th Infantry, and the 22nd Infantry, all of which had been formed during the Civil War.

The Badge of the 11th Infantry was the white Maltese cross. The 18th Infantry had a red acorn for its Badge. The 22nd Infantry was famous for defending Vicksburg when it was under siege. The blue square represents a fort and the indentations are supposed to represent defensive positions. When the 35th was formed all these elements were combined to create our regiment crest. And that's what you're looking at on this sign."

"Okay, I guess I get it now. But you still haven't told my why this cactus is blue instead of green."

"The regiment grew large enough that it needed to be divided into two battalions. The First Battalion has a green cactus. The Second Battalion has a blue cactus."

The Sergeant had finished his cigarette and his history lesson. He got up and started out of the tent.

"But a blue cactus?"

"Just paint the sign."

The next two days were spent carefully going over the sign with new paint until it glistened like new. I not only was proud of my accomplishment but was happy that I was out of sight of NCOs looking for new meat to do all the other mindless projects that were under way.

C-RATIONS AND PUFF THE MAGIC DRAGON

My squad leader teamed me up with a veteran soldier who would soon be going home. He had been drafted and had no plans to reenlist. The quiet, black PFC seemed both amused and annoyed at my inexperience. I had been an Eagle Scout with a lot of camping experience. And I had completed both Basic Combat Training and Advanced Infantry Training. Most of my training and experience was useless out here. He showed me how to burn plastic explosives to heat my C-rations, what to pack on patrol and what to leave behind, and how to take care of myself in the jungle. I learned how to coax leeches off my body with the hot end of a cigarette or melt them with mosquito repellant. Toilet paper and cigarettes didn't get so soaked as to be unusable if carried strapped to my helmet. We wouldn't be having tents, cots, sleeping bags, or other such comforts, so I learned to pick out where I would lay down before dark. I would clear it of roots, pebbles, and make sure it wasn't on an anthill. After two weeks, my teacher told me that he was heading back to the world. He had to explain to me that "going back to the world" meant that he was leaving Viet Nam---and the Army. I was on my own.

Becoming part of A Company was not easy. Most of the other guys had known each other for years. They had worked and trained together in Hawaii and were very comfortable with each other. Every one had proven to the other that they could be trusted under fire. And then there were us replacements! None of us had been under fire. All the original guys were trained Jungle Warfare Experts; most of us were just out of Advanced Infantry Training. Jimmy Hill was a Staff Sergeant who had pulled one tour in Korea. I had spent my first year in Germany as a security guard for an ordnance company. The rest had been in the Army less than a year.

Until this point in my career, my meals had been prepared for me by cooks and usually served in a mess hall. On those rare occasions when I wasn't near a mess hall, hot food had been prepared, delivered and served. Since A Company spent so much time out on operations, my diet now consisted mainly of something called C-Rations. C-Rations, officially named Meal, Combat, Individual, were basically canned meals in a box. A case of meals would contain 12 meals. There would be four can openers in a case. These tiny can openers, called P-38's, had a blade that folded away from the rest of the device at a 90 degree angle, and with some experience and effort, would allow one to open the cans. A hole at one corner made a convenient attachment point so the P-38 could be worn on the dog tag chain. Each individual meal came packaged in a cardboard box. Included would be a canned meat item, something with fruit involved, and either a bread or dessert. A foil pouch containing individual servings of cigarettes, matches, chewing gum, toilet paper, coffee, cream, sugar, and salt was also included. A plastic spoon completed the package. Each meal provided approximately 1,200 calories.

There were even choices of meat. Of course, the choices were pretty random. You might get beef steak, chopped ham and eggs, ham slices, or turkey loaf. These weren't too bad heated but were downright nasty cold. These rations were later replaced by a "choice" of beans and wieners, spaghetti and meatballs, beefsteak with potatoes and gravy, ham and lima beans, or meatballs and beans. Except for the ham and lima beans, these were all good heated. The beefsteak wasn't edible cold. The ham and lima beans meal just wasn't fit for human consumption whatever you did to it!

The fruit was always good and might be applesauce, fruit cocktail, peaches, or pears. On a lucky day there would be a chocolate bar, a fruit cake, or a pound cake. The biggest prize of all, however, would be a package of powdered cocoa. By itself, it wasn't much, but if you had been saving your sugar and cream packets for this special day, a gourmet treat was in store when you found time to heat this concoction up and sit back to enjoy. Did I mention bread? Just kidding---- unless you can consider stale crackers to be a bread. Sometimes a processed cheese spread would be provided to make the saltines a little more palatable.

When we stopped in one place long enough to clear a landing zone out of the jungle for helicopters to land, hot meals were flown out to us. These meals were much better than our standard fare of C-rations but usually didn't compare with the meals being regularly served back at base camp. A real treat did surface on one occasion, however.

We had been set up as a Company size base of operations for about a week. Platoons took turns every day performing a patrol of the surrounding area while the other two platoons stayed at the base camp. A small landing area for helicopters had been cleared and minor fortifications were in place. Our camp was on a hilltop from where we could view the surrounding jungle. This was truly a beautiful country except for the natives who wanted to kill us.

I was manning a position on the perimeter when the daily supply helicopter arrived. As soon as the cargo was unloaded, the helicopter flew off. The four insulated, olive drab containers were sure indicators that our hot chow had arrived. The Sergeant in charge of the work detail had the containers set up in a row in preparation for serving dinner. He opened the lid on the first container and quickly turned to look at the departing supply ship. Slamming the lid shut, he moved to inspect the contents of the other containers. A broad smile covered his face. It was the first time I had ever seen this man smile.

"Everybody---Come get this chow!! Now! Leave one man guarding each direction. Move it! Come on!"

I couldn't understand what all the excitement was about. It was probably something like beef stew with boiled potatoes. Once served, however, I got excited too. Steaks! Mashed potatoes and gravy! Oyster dressing! And—unbelievably—ice cream! We gobbled down huge portions as if we would never eat again while the old Sergeant scanned the sky looking for something.

By the time the supply helicopter made his return, we had scraped the containers bare. Not a crumb was left to be loaded back. Empty containers and smiling faces were the only evidence of the feast.

The Sergeant and the pilot had a heated discussion. The helicopter left with the pilot wondering how he was going to explain how the Colonel's meal got delivered to us by mistake.

Some of the older guys were more open than the rest. Fourtney and Chace were both machine-gunners and pretty friendly. Chace loved to talk about cars and how he could fix them up to go faster. Fourtney was one of the old guys who sort of took me under his wing. He was bigger than most of us, muscular and agile. He entertained us with stories that he had been a stunt man in the movies. Westerns, mostly. He was assigned as machine-gunner, but it wasn't a bit unusual to find him at my side whenever I was on point trying to crash a trail through a seemingly impenetrable patch of jungle. Sergeant Rivera, the Platoon Sergeant, was probably the most welcoming. In the evenings, when we didn't have duty, many of us would flock around him like admiring kindergarteners sitting at the feet of their teacher. The wiry Mexican was all business while on duty, but we all knew instinctively that he really cared for every one of us.

One evening after mail call Sergeant Rivera was sharing news from home. He had recently paid off his house and had a picture of it. It was a very modest looking ranch-style house. It didn't look like much from the picture, but it had to be nicer than the old farmhouse I had grown up in. We had only been tenants and he owned his free and clear.

"Yes, boys, two more years and I will retire to my casa. I will go nowhere except the market. I will sit on my porch and enjoy my retrement."

"Retirement", corrected Clendenon. "The word is retirement, not retrement."

Chuck Clendenon and Art Johnson had come together to the Company shortly after I had. Chuck was a very personable guy from California. He had made friends quickly and really was very intelligent. But here he was—a Private-- just matter-of–factly correcting the veteran Platoon Sergeant! A hush fell over us as we watched Sergeant Rivera ponder his thoughts for awhile. Finally and suddenly he was grinning broadly.

"Thank you so very much! My English, it is not so good. Thank you."

We were soon joined by Chace and Fourtney. A large plane lumbered along in the distance. Cargo planes didn't usually fly at night over our area.

"Watch this!" said Fourtney. "It's Puff! I can tell by the sound."

"Puff" puzzled Rodebaugh. "What the hell's a Puff?"

"Puff The Magic Dragon. Watch and learn."

"It's really called Spooky", corrected Chace. "People just call him Puff."

The oversized plane settled into a slow bank and began circling an area of the sky. Suddenly flames seemed to burst out of the plane. It looked like three streams of fire coming from the plane almost to the ground. The flames stopped briefly and then began again.

"Tracers" beamed Fourtney. "He's got three mini-guns that can shoot 100 rounds a second ---each!"

"Yeah" added Chace. "And he can put a bullet every square yard. Wish I could shoot that accurately!"

Then we heard the rumbling roar. The sound of the three guns rapidly firing that many rounds echoed from the nearly empty cargo area of the plane.

"Damn!" said Waycaster. "It does sound like a dragon or sumthin!"

We sat in awe for several minutes watching Spooky or Puff or whatever you wanted to call him rain down death on the enemy. Then as quickly as he had appeared he was gone.

"Guess the show's over for the night", stated Fourtney as he picked himself up and wandered off to the perimeter.

Chace left right behind him. The rest of us just sat there for awhile, trying to digest what we had just witnessed. None of us had ever seen such a raw display of firepower.

"I'm just glad he's on our side" remarked Rodebaugh as we all left for our respective places on the perimeter.

AMBUSHES AND MALARIA

The first of August we began Operation Paul Revere II. That didn't mean a whole lot to us grunts except that we now had an official name for the operation we were on. The boundaries for our operation were the Cambodian border to the west, Highway Route 14 to the east, and two imaginary grid lines to the north and south. This gave us an area of about approximately 2040 square miles to be responsible for. That's a lot of jungle, rivers, and mountains! We were supposed to maintain surveillance of the Cambodian border, conduct ambushes, and otherwise prevent the enemy from penetrating our assigned area. No small task!

The way we approached covering such a large area was to use a process known as "checker-boarding". The entire area of operation was divided up into square grids of 10,000 square meters. Units could easily be moved from one grid to another. Exact locations could readily be pin-pointed. But, again, that's something the people in charge decided. The grunts only knew one thing for certain-- today we're here (wherever "here" is) and tomorrow we'll probably be someplace else!

August was a month of gradual increase of contact with the enemy. They seemed to be increasing in numbers. As many as five North Vietnamese regiments were supposed to be in our area of operations. That could be somewhere around 5,000 well trained and equipped enemy soldiers! We searched hard for them, but only found groups of 100 or less. When we did locate them and make contact, they would quickly break contact and disappear. They seemed to be waiting for just the right situation before committing to any kind of serious confrontation with us. That didn't bother us in the field nearly as badly as it did Headquarters. Everywhere we went it seemed that there were eyes on us. Every once in a while the spies would be spotted, shot at, and then they would just disappear. This went on through out August and September.

We were in the rainy season called the monsoon season. It seemed to always be raining. When it wasn't raining, the sun would come out and add even more humidity to air that was already saturated. Wearing a poncho didn't help to keep our bodies dry since it was so humid. The poncho did add some warmth at night when it cooled off somewhat. This was rain beyond description. It was almost like being underwater. No place in Viet Nam gets as much rain during monsoon season as the Central Highland area around Pleiku. We couldn't have found the enemy unless we just happened to walk into each other.

We tried ambushes with little effect. My first ambush attempt was well prepared. Some South Vietnamese troops had been in contact earlier in the day. They had killed two enemy soldiers before both sides retreated. Knowing that the enemy would return after dark to retrieve their fallen comrades, we decided to set an ambush. We picked up extra ammunition, hand grenades, and claymore mines. Positions were carefully plotted for the maximum effect. Everybody carried an empty sandbag. The plan for the sandbags left me a little unsettled. After the ambush we were to quickly search any enemy we killed and put all their possessions in the sandbags. What a very cold and disrespectful thing to do! I tried to picture myself going through the pockets of a dead man. I wasn't sure I could.

At dusk we moved to the ambush site. The bodies were still there, lying in the middle of the trail. As silently as we could we moved into position. There were four of us located in a position together. Two would watch while the other two slept. I had second watch so I went a few yards to the rear and settled down next to a tree. Unable to really sleep, knowing that at any minute the enemy could show up, I did doze off and on enough to feel rested before my turn at watch arrived.

As quietly as we could we changed positions with the team members coming off guard. I took note of where they settled in. One of them liked my place beside the tree and the other lay down beside a large rock a few yards away. I clicked the safety switch off on my rifle and returned my attention back to the trail in front of me.

Time really drags at night in the jungle. It seemed like hours had gone by before I dug my watch out of my pocket. One o'clock. I had begun watch at midnight. Has my watch stopped? This constantly humid climate had all but destroyed the timepiece I had paid a lot of money for before leaving Germany. The expanding metal band had rusted quickly and disintegrated after only a month. A cloud of moisture fogged the inside of the crystal. After a while I dug it back out of my pocket and looked again. One-fifteen. I'm beginning to wonder if these guys are going to show up at all.

The commotion behind me took us all completely by surprise. When I first heard movement back there I assumed that somebody was just answering the call of nature. Then there was some shouting---some scuffling----a shot-----some more shots. Everybody involved in the ambush was now focused on the area directly behind me.

The enemy had returned for their dead, not up the path in front of us as we had expected, but from our rear. The man who had taken my place under the tree was sound asleep with his poncho pulled over his head. The enemy litter bearer must have thought that the GI was one of the bodies he had been sent to retrieve. When he pulled the poncho back, the GI sat upright immediately. The GI screamed and the enemy screamed back. At this point it was a toss-up as to who was scared the most. A brief wrestling match ended with the enemy getting a shot off with his carbine, wounding the GI in the leg. The enemy then fled under a hail of gunfire.

With the element of surprise gone, the ambush was over. We returned to the Company area with our wounded man. I returned the sandbag to the pile where I picked it up, empty.

Life in the jungle was miserable even without the fear of getting killed or wounded. We carried no shelter other than a poncho.

We used rocks and logs for furniture. Ten paces from our foxhole was the latrine, but you had to dig your own individual hole each time. During the monsoon season we could strip down and bathe in the rain. Otherwise we settled for washing to the best of our ability using our helmets for washbasins. Clean uniforms might come once a week if we were lucky. Three giant-sized bags would arrive-one bag of shirts, one bag of trousers, and one bag of socks. We would take turns digging through the bags until we found something that came close to fitting. I had quit even trying to wear underwear. Snakes, large lizards, tarantula spiders, leeches, and biting ants were always present. The mosquitoes were always hungry and seemed to like me a lot.

Malaria was a major concern. It seemed like every day or so somebody was either leaving or returning to the unit because of malaria. We were given a daily pill by the medic that was supposed to keep us from coming down with it. The pill was pretty effective---if we took it. Most of us would prefer to contract malaria than be out in the field. Some of us threw the pill away. I was one of those.

Doc Molohon, the medic, became very serious about our malaria pills. He even reached the point where he personally watched us take our pill. The night after he cracked down, I realized his efforts were too late for me.

It began with a fever and a pounding headache. I thought my head was going to explode! Then, just as suddenly as the fever had come on it left me. The problem was that the fever was immediately replaced with the chills! I was shivering in the tropical heat. Then the chills were gone and the fever and headache returned. I was sweating profusely. Every muscle in my body ached. Then the chills and shakes came back. What had I done to myself? I suffered through the night and in the morning was flown out to the hospital.

After the first day in the hospital I felt I might live after all. Every day I got better and stronger. My biggest problem was the frequent taking of blood samples. The tip of every one of my fingers was sore from being pricked four or five times a day.

Wandering around the hospital, I met guys from all over. Davenport had been one of the original guys who came with A Company from Hawaii. I had heard about him from the other guys in the Company. He had owned a car when most of the others didn't and often gave rides back and forth to town when they had passes. He had somehow managed to get reassigned to some Special Forces group as a truck driver.

I met two guys who had enlisted together on the "Buddy System." They were guaranteed to stay together the entire time of their enlistment. I asked them the most common ice-breaking question.

"How long have you been in the hospital?"

"Going on three months now."

"Three months! Wow! What in the world happened to you guys?"

I was amazed that they had been around here so long. Most of us would be here for one or two weeks, a month at the most. Guys with more serious problems were sent to larger hospitals, usually out of the country.

"We came in for malaria. Hung around as long as we could. Now we've been circumcised."

"Circumcised!?!? What in the world?"

"We got the idea while talking to the Priest. Somehow the topic came up and we shared with him that we'd never had it done. He made the arrangements and here we are."

"Are you all that religious?"

"Not really, but we can't go back out into the field until we're all healed. You know-- infections and such."

I understood all too well wanting a valid reason for staying out of the field, but circumcision? Mine had been done as an infant, so it wasn't even an option for me. I doubt I would have suffered through that to stay out of the field.

Life in the hospital was very plush compared to the regular life of a grunt in the field. Wearing clean, dry clothes and being able to stay clean were two of the greatest perks. Throw in three hot meals a day and a comfortable bed to sleep in at night and I was as close to Heaven as one could get while on Earth. Then we got the word that Nancy Sinatra was coming.

Nancy Sinatra, daughter of the legendary Frank Sinatra, had come into her own in the past year or so. A brassy singer, her hit song "These Boots Were Made for Walking" was very popular, especially among the Infantry guys. Now I would have the opportunity to see her entertain in person! This had to be one of the greatest treats of my life.

The big day arrived and there we were in the grass covered amphitheater ready to be entertained. Thousands of young men covered every square inch of the ground. The American women who sang and danced to begin the show stirred up the hormonally charged crowd. Then Nancy herself appeared wearing a mini-skirt and her signature boots.

The crowd was quiet as she started the show with her newest hit song, "Sugartown".

"I've got some problems, but they won't last.
I'm gonna lay right down here in the grass.
And pretty soon all my troubles will pass—
I'll be in Su-Su-Su,Su-SuSu,Su-Su-Su-Su-Su-Sugar Town"

The crowd erupted with cheers and cat-calls. All the young bucks were fired up just being close to so many attractive young women. I stole a glance at the two buddies who had so recently had their circumcisions. They appeared to be in pain, pulling and adjusting their crotches.

All good things must come to an end. The show ended and a couple days later I found myself loaded in the back of a two and a half ton truck with twenty or so other soldiers being returned to their various units for duty. It was a very long ride to Pleiku. It was now the dry season. The same dirt that was gooey mud a month ago now billowed into huge red clouds of dust that threatened to choke our breath away. By the time we arrived at the base camp we were all caked with the dirt. The only way we could tell each other apart was by our nametags.

The very next day I found myself back in the field with A Company.

In the hospital with malaria

LET'S GO TO TOWN

During September we got to guard a bridge. This was really great duty. All the fortifications were already in place. They had walls of sandbags stacked four bags thick. Heavy timbers supported a sandbag roof. Having these strong fortifications felt much safer than the shallow holes we had been scraping out of the ground every night. In addition, a platoon of four tanks was also assigned to the position. Somebody evidently felt that this bridge was very valuable!

We set up a defensive position and just watched the people go by. As they smiled at us we couldn't help but know that these same smiling faces turned into deadly enemies at night. Many of these people were offering services—anything from prostitutes to women wanting to do our laundry. Since I only had the clothes I was wearing I gave one lady my poncho liner to wash. She took it down to the river and worked furiously on it for over an hour. As I watched her from my position on the bridge it was really obvious that she really needed to make some honest money. She came back carrying the still dingy poncho liner and shaking her head. It was much cleaner than when she had started. I was happy to pay her for her efforts.

One morning after a rain, Waycaster was beginning to get bored. He watched with fascination as the local taxis navigated the hill on the ether side of the bridge. The taxis were nothing but a small motorcycle with a large box built on the back of it. Four to six people would sit on bench seats on either side of the motorcycle. Needless to say, the taxis were sorely overloaded. If they got a running start, they could make it to the top of the hill—but not without great difficulty.

He was suddenly inspired.

"Hey Ya'll—watch this1" he beamed.

Waiting until the taxi was just about to the top of the hill, he jumped on the back. His weight, plus the weight of the passengers raised the motorcycle completely off the ground. With no engine to propel the taxi forward, it slid all the way back to the bottom of the hill. Waycaster then jumped off amid a torrent of what had to be some of the worse cursing possible in the Vietnamese language.

Not wanting to be outdone, Rodebaugh jumped on the taxi during its second attempt up the hill. By now the passengers and the driver were livid. It was great fun for awhile, but we decided it wasn't doing a lot of good for public relations.

On the first of October, we returned to the Brigade Base Camp at Pleiku for "refitting and retraining". Later on these periods of rest from the field were called "Stand Downs". Weapons were cleaned, uniforms repaired or replaced, and personnel records were brought up to date. We got some rest from the field and had a chance to catch up on our mail.

New camouflage covers for our steel helmets were being issued. My cover was worn, dirty, and rotten. It also was just plain olive drab in color. We were all jealous of the "tiger stripe" camouflage uniforms we had seen Special Forces and South Korean troops wearing. We were finally getting some camouflage! The broad grins quickly turned to frowns and looks of disbelief once the crate was opened. They were indeed camouflaged. The thing that puzzled us all was the bright blue cactus plant embroidered on the right side.

"Cacti Blue!" beamed the Supply Sergeant. "You all know that's our Regiment Crest".

"What---didn't anybody around there know how to draw a bull's-eye?" Wise cracked Rodebaugh. "That's gonna make a hell of a fine target in the jungle!"

"That shouldn't matter none to you. It ain't like you're gonna sneak up on nobody nohow, unless they think you're a water buffalo." taunted Waycaster.

We fussed and fumed for awhile about the gaudy covers. Somebody much higher than us in the food chain obviously thought they were impressive. We weren't impressed at all. Most of us had already ripped our old covers off and thrown them away in anticipation. Now we had no choice but to wear the new covers. Finally Clendenon spoke up.

"Look you guys, it doesn't matter. We all carry so much junk on our helmets, that cactus plant isn't going to make any difference."

He was right, of course. We never wore the chin strap around our chins. Instead, it was left folded up on the helmet. That made it a convenient place to carry C-ration toilet paper and cigarettes, both of which soon turned into soggy messes if kept in a pocket. If a bottle of mosquito repellant leaked in a pocket you would end up with a nasty chemical burn on your skin, so it would often be attached to the helmet also. Then there was the occasional peace sign, home town, or motto written with permanent marker. No, a blue cactus wouldn't make any difference. But I still found the first convenient mud hole and rendered it not quite so glaring. I should have just packed it away somewhere since they were never issued again.

Shortly after I was assigned a permanent mailing address, I received a letter from my Grandmother. It had contained a self-addressed, stamped envelope, two pieces of writing paper, and a pencil. The enclosed note said simply "Write Me!" She was always straight to the point and allowed no excuses. I found her letters first in my stack of mail and promptly answered them. I sure didn't want her down on me.

That chore completed, I could focus on the rest of my mail. Letters from my Mother, sisters, cousins, and aunts were all read and savored. It really felt good to know that all these people cared for me enough to take time out of their busy lives to drop me a note. I even got a letter from my local draft board once informing me that I was to report. When I quit laughing, I replied that I would gladly report if they would provide transportation. I never got a reply so I assume they figured it out.

I was down to my last piece of mail. It was from my fiancé's mother. Her daughter, Elaine, and I had been with each other for two years now. Elaine had wanted to get married when I returned from Germany, but I wasn't really ready, and my parents wouldn't sign for me anyway. I also knew that I wasn't her mother's first choice for a son-in-law. That's why it was so puzzling to receive a letter from this lady.

I unfolded and read the letter.

Dear Curt,

I wanted to tell you this before you heard it from somewhere else. Elaine got married last week. It was a beautiful ceremony. You have no reason to come back here.

I knew several guys who had received a "Dear John" letter. I'm sure getting one from the girl's mother put me in a very small minority. I sat in silence, reading the short and not so sweet letter over and over again. Maybe I had read it wrong. Did I miss something? How could this be? Unbelievable! I had received a letter from Elaine just two weeks ago. She had to have been in the middle of her wedding plans as she wrote. How would I ever survive this?

Fourtney showed up not long after I read the letter. He had Rodebaugh and Waycaster with him.

"What you doing sitting around here?"

" I dunno, why?"

"We're going to town, that's why. Come on, the truck's getting ready to leave."

Ready for a diversion, I laid my rifle on my bunk and headed out.

"Now what the hell do you think you're doing? Pick that rifle up and come on."

"Take my gun to town? That sounds like something from a country-western song!"

"Look-- you're Infantry. You don't leave your rifle anywhere. I thought you knew that by now."

I really hadn't noticed at first, but they were all armed. Waycaster and Rodebaugh both had their rifles, and Fortney was wearing a pistol belt with his Army 45 pistol on one side and a revolver on the other side. His ensemble was accented with a hand grenade beside each pistol.

It was a short, bumpy ride down Dragon Mountain into the town of Pleiku. As we went downhill I could see Artillery Hill to my right. I had never been up there but I had heard the big guns going off all day and most of the night. There was an Air Force base around here somewhere also. I'm sure there was a lot of military stationed in the area that I was unaware of. I hadn't even fully explored our own base camp.

Even with the canvas side curtains in place on the two and a half ton truck the red dust still rolled around us and settled into every possible cavity of our bodies. The truck screeched to a halt in a parking lot about a block away from the main business district.

The town of Pleiku was not really what one would call a tourist attraction. It is located at the intersection of the only two major roads in the Central Highlands, Routes 19 and 14. Route 14 leads north to the town of Kon Tum, only a short distance from North Vietnam. To the south Route 14 goes to Boum Ma Thout then turns west towards Cambodia and a safe haven for the North Vietnamese Army. Route 19 runs east and west, from Cambodia again to Qui Nhon on the Vietnamese coast. The city is centered on a deep ravine where an artificial lake has been created. The city is a market center for the surrounding area. The American military is centered here for obvious strategic reasons. Most travelers, however, are just passing through. The major thoroughfares are crowded with noisy traffic all day, and the streets are lined with stores that mostly specialize in selling goods in bulk. Merchants and buyers were noisily engaged in the negotiating and bickering over prices that is a part of this commercial culture.

"The last truck back leaves at 4:00 sharp", announced the driver to nobody in particular as he dropped the tailgate with a bang. "Be here."

We all climbed out and stood looking around. I had never been to Pleiku before. Calling it a town was a real stretch of the imagination. The narrow streets were not paved, just packed down hard from years of use. There were no sidewalks. People wandered about attending to their business. It wasn't a bit unusual to see a woman move off the side of the road and pull the leg of her baggy, pajama-type trousers up to her crotch. After squatting and relieving herself she would just stand and continue on her way. Oh well! When nature calls, it calls. Aside from the always present military vehicles, the only vehicles were motorcycles and bicycles. No cars. An occasional cart with wooden wheels and drawn by a water buffalo dominated the road. The buildings were all either wooden or made of bamboo. Sometimes sheet metal, originally intended to be cut up as beer or soda drink cans, was used for siding or roofing.

It was easy to tell which establishments catered to military--- they were the only ones with signs written in English.

One sign in particular grabbed our attention—"American Food---Beer---Girls". It drew us inside like a magnet in a pile of metal shavings. It took a few seconds for our eyes to adjust to the dimly lit interior. Incense was burning somewhere. Soothing oriental music was playing quietly. We seemed to have the place to ourselves so we took over one of the six wooden tables that occupied one corner of the room. A large bar ran the length of the wall opposite of the door. Six young girls eagerly watched us from their perches along the bar.

An older woman stood behind the bar, grinning at us through stained teeth.

Once we settled into a table, the older woman came over to us. "I'm Mama-San. What you likey?"

Seeing that we new guys didn't have a clue, Fourtney spoke for the group. "Bring us some cold beer for starters. American beer. "

" You wanty food?"

"Not yet. Just some beer for now."

Mama-San left us for the bar, shooting a go-ahead look towards the girls as she passed them.

Before Mama-San could return with our drinks, the girls had swarmed our table. Except for the different colored dresses they wore, I couldn't tell them apart. None weighed more than a hundred pounds. The one with the blue dress with white flowers slid onto my lap.

"You buy me tea, GI? Only 50 P."

P was short for Piaster, the local currency. 50 P was about 50 cents. That was a pricy cup of tea, since my beer was only 25 P. But the girls couldn't stay unless we kept buying those drinks. We were all craving company and really had no place else to spend our money.

"Sure, let's have a party."

The beer and tea had been flowing pretty well for about an hour when the Military Police made their appearance. The two Sergeants stood in the doorway for awhile, turned just enough sideways that everybody could see their black armbands with the white letters "MP". They spoke to each other in hushed tones as they looked us over.

Fourtney was rocked back in his chair, perched on its two rear legs. The girl in the red dress was sitting in his lap, facing him and whispering in his ear. One of Fourtney's hands held a beer and the other hand rested on his civilian 45 pistol. Waycaster was sighting his rifle at some imaginary target on the ceiling. Rodebaugh rolled a hand grenade back and forth between his hands while green dress stood behind him with her arms around his neck.

After a short discussion, the MPs went to the other side of the room, where two Air Force guys wearing civilian clothes were sitting. My guess is that they were just tired of always being in uniform. It was really unlikely that they actually thought they would be able to blend in with the civilians. The MPs made them show ID and gave one a hard time about the 38 caliber pistol he had stuck in his belt. The Air Force guys protested and pointed across the room to where we were sitting. The MPs then left without even glancing back in our direction.

Not long after that I had to leave. I was already drunk and not very good company to anybody, especially to myself. The words of the Dear John letter still stung at my heart. I was angry and sad at the same time. The empty, lonely feeling would not go away unless it got pushed aside by the anger of betrayal.

BIRTHDAYS AND OTHER BAD DAYS

On the tenth day of October we were back in the field again guarding a section of Highway 19. I could get used to this kind of duty. Some of us thought it was boring to sit around guarding bridges all day. Some of us thought boring was good. Nights, however, were kind of edgy. Listening posts were sent out in all directions as a precaution. It wasn't unusual to hear people bypassing the bridges at night and forging the stream. We never saw anybody. Was it the enemy or was it civilians afraid of being shot if they approached the bridge after dark? We never went to find out. Our little gravy train only lasted about a week this time. A Company was moving out to the jungle again.

"Saddle Up!"

Rest time was over. It was October 21. Yesterday had been my Birthday. I was now twenty years old. There was no celebration for me except that I was alive and well. We had begun Operation Paul Revere IV four days ago. I wondered how many Operation Paul Reveres we would have before I got to go home.

The heavy load I was carrying strained at my back and shoulders as I stood with the rest of the Third Platoon waiting for the helicopters. Including all my gear, ammunition, and weapon I was carrying about sixty pounds. No wonder we were referred to as "grunts". When the choppers arrived we fought the sand blowing in our faces as we ran stooped over to climb aboard. I had never ridden in a helicopter before I came to Viet Nam. As it lifted slowly off the ground, the rocking motion reminded me of a Ferris wheel ride. Once we reached a certain altitude we seemed to pause for just a second before tilting forward slightly. Then we were off to our destination--- wherever that was.

Soon all five choppers were flying over the jungle in a tight formation. There was a door gunner at each door. Each gunner was seated in a chair made of webbing with an M-60 machine gun mounted almost in his lap.

Looking over the shoulder of the nearest gunner, I could look out over the lush canopy of the jungle. What a beautiful place this was, I silently marveled. It was such a sharp contrast to the flat, treeless prairie of Illinois where I had grown up.

After fifteen or twenty minutes we were at the landing zone. We jumped out both doors into the tall elephant grass and quickly formed a tight perimeter. The choppers lifted off and disappeared, leaving A Company on their own.

The officers went into a brief huddle before sprinting to their respective platoons. My Platoon Leader, Lieutenant Lugo, was the first officer I had ever seen with a star above his Combat Infantry Badge, which represented having earned two CIBs. He had been in the Dominican Republic during that brief action. That amount of experience in a junior officer was rare and gave us a lot of confidence in his leadership ability. The Lieutenant issued orders to his NCOs and in a matter of seconds Sergeant Bailey was giving direction.

"OK, Third Herd, lead out. Waycaster, you're on point. Gay left flank. Hernandez, right flank. Let's go."

He pointed to the mountain that loomed in the distance beyond the jungle.

Waycaster and Hernandez were as green as me. While we had been part of A Company for almost three months now, we were still the new guys. And the new guys always got to walk the point and flank positions.

Waycaster disappeared into the jungle. He was more at home in the woods than any other man in the Company. Growing up in the mountains of West Virginia gave him a distinct advantage over the rest of us. His wiry frame slid through the jungle as if it wasn't there. Hernandez and I, however, weren't faring as well. There weren't many woods where I grew up, and Hernandez was a city boy from Aqua

Buenos, Puerto Rico. Our crashing through the jungle had to send a loud message that we were coming.

A message came over the radio. We were all allowed to pause while the Lieutenant took the mike from the radio operator. He looked puzzled at first. After asking the person at the other end of the airwaves to repeat, he appeared agitated and even angry. He paused for a long minute, staring at the mike. What in the world could it be? We were all concerned. The Lieutenant took a deep breath to control his frustration.

"Okay. 'They' want to know how many of us voted in the last election."

It would have been funny if it weren't so ironic! We were a bunch of kids! Our average age was 19. Only Lieutenant Lugo and Chace were even old enough to vote. The Lieutenant composed himself long enough to report his informal poll and we were on our way again. About an hour later we reached the base of the mountain. Hernandez and I were called in from the flanks. The Company split up by Platoons. Everybody else would move around the mountain to the left and to the right. Third Platoon would climb straight up from where we were. A short lunch break was taken before starting the climb.

Waycaster led the way up the mountain, closely followed by Gene Johnson. Hernandez and I were next, trying to keep up. The climb would have been demanding even without all the gear we were carrying. Every time we thought we were coming to the summit it turned out to be only a ledge hiding the rest of the mountain from view. I had just about decided that there was no end to the climb when Waycaster and Johnson disappeared over the summit. They were kneeling and pointing their rifles to the flanks like a human gate as I hurried through between them. After moving forward about thirty yards, I assumed a kneeling firing position with Rodebaugh moving up beside me doing the same. Together we surveyed the jungle in front of us while the rest of the Platoon completed the ascent.

As soon as the entire Platoon was on top we were on the move again. This time it was me and Rodebaugh leading the way. The jungle was very open here, more like a forest. The canopy of trees prevented us from seeing the sky. The vegetation on the ground consisted mostly of scattered shrubs.

The strong smell of garlic was in the air. That was always a warning that the enemy was near. Two huge pots of rice were cooking on open fires. Twenty small shelters surrounded the cooking area. The shelters were shallow pits with small branches cut and placed in rows for a roof. Most had clothing and blankets still inside. Nobody seemed to be around the camp at the moment. A well traveled trail led out of the camp and down the opposite slope.

We moved forward, searching both sides of the trail. Private Bailey, no relation to the Sergeant, suddenly flopped on the ground thirty feet ahead of me.

"There goes one," he screamed, pointing to our right. I moved up beside him.

"Where? I don't see anything."

"Straight ahead! He's in those bushes! Shoot him!" Sixty feet ahead of us was a sizable clump of brush. I hadn't seen anybody before and didn't see anybody now, but that didn't mean an enemy soldier wasn't hiding there.

I sprayed the brush with my rifle, firing on full automatic until I had covered every square inch.

"Is that where you meant?"

"Yeah, that's good! You got him! You got him!"

Cautiously, we got up and moved forward, keeping our weapons aimed at the brush. If there had been anybody there, they were gone now. I believed that Bailey was just seeing things until others started shooting at fleeing enemy soldiers. Probably twenty or so were spotted in small groups fleeing the area. Feeling that the enemy was definitely on the run, the Platoon left the rear area of the base camp in a column. As we moved down the trail we discovered some fortifications at the front of the area that were facing down the slope. The plan was to occupy these and continue searching the area. All the positions faced downhill. They hadn't prepared for anybody to come from the direction we had taken.

I was in the middle of the squad this time, following the machine-gun crew. My thoughts went back to this morning-that seems like an eternity ago-while we were waiting for the choppers to arrive. I had the strangest conversation with Chace, the squad machine-gunner. Chace was usually a quiet guy but this morning he had wanted to talk.

"This is my Birthday."

"Really? Mine was yesterday. How old are you?"

"I'm twenty-three today. It's too bad I'm going to die today."

"What do you mean?" I was met with a cold stare.

"I'm going to die today.."

"What are you talking about?"

"When I woke up this morning I knew it would be the last time I would see the sun rise."

"That's crazy!"

"I know."

The Platoon approached the face of the slope with Waycaster and Rodebaugh sharing the lead. Suddenly two North Vietnamese soldiers appeared on the trail with their hands raised in the air and looking very scared. They were yelling something in Vietnamese.

"They want to surrender!" yelled the Lieutenant. "Move up and secure them."

Waycaster and Rodebaugh cautiously approached them. Most of us had never seen the enemy in the flesh before.

Before the prisoners could be secured automatic weapon fire came from every direction. We had been tricked into an ambush! Diving for cover, we returned fire. Automatic weapon fire was coming from at least four locations plus single shot fire from several others. Hand grenades fell in the middle of our group and exploded, adding to the intensity of the attack.

We were able to respond quickly. We fired our weapons as we moved off the trail. A hasty perimeter was established. Somebody out there seemed to be paying particular attention to me. I'd shoot and he would shoot back. He suddenly stopped shooting. Was it over? No. A quick check to my left and right confirmed that everybody else was still fighting. Where was my guy? I raised high enough to take a peek. I saw him! He was trying to get in closer. He would jump up, run five feet, and then dive back down.

Another sixty feet and he would be on top of me! As I looked down the length of my rifle barrel he jumped up again. I lined up the target with both my front and rear sights. I squeezed the trigger. His rifle flew out of his hands. His arms jerked out straight in front of his body. He fell to the ground on his face.

What had just happened? I just killed somebody! That wasn't a target on a training range. Did I just take a life? My stomach drew up in a tight knot as I reloaded. I was relieved to see nothing moving when I looked in front of me again.

Lieutenant Lugo was yelling into the radio as he called for support. It wasn't long before he had artillery firing around us. Then I heard the plane. The Lieutenant ordered his Sergeants to mark our location with smoke grenades. We all got as low to the ground as we possibly could as Puff did his thing. We had all seen the AC-47 aircraft, nicknamed Puff the Magic Dragon or Spooky, in operation from a distance, but I was totally unprepared for what happened next. The jungle in front of me was being shredded to pieces as Puff fired hundreds of bullets in just seconds. I didn't hear the guns fire until after the entire area in front of me had been reduced to splinters. An hour of fierce fighting was over in seconds with the help of Puff. The plane was gone as suddenly as it had appeared. It had broken the back of our enemy.

Once we were sure that the fight was over, we reorganized back into our regular squads. When the battle had begun everybody had taken up position wherever they could find cover with little or no regard for order and structure.

The rest of the Company soon arrived. It was time to make a search of the battlefield. Emotions crowded in as I prepared to move forward. The man I shot would be out there. The thought of looking at the dead body of somebody I had killed really bothered me. I prepared myself for the moment as I cautiously approached the area where he fell.

He was gone! I hadn't missed. Blood was everywhere. Had he crawled off? Had his comrades dragged his body away? I don't know.

The sweep of the area yielded four wounded enemy, several automatic weapons, about a hundred foxholes, and a light anti-aircraft position with the gun still intact. Large amounts of rice and new uniforms were also discovered. Quite a haul!

But it was not without a price. As he had predicted, Chace had been killed in the battle.

Darkness was starting to settle in as the Company occupied the positions that the enemy had carefully prepared. The enemy machine gun that had killed Chace was placed in Rodebaugh's possession.

"Hope I get a chance to blow the bastards apart with their own damned gun", he growled.

After a dinner of cold C-rations we settled in for a long night of guard duty. Sergeant Bailey assigned me to the position with Rodebaugh. It overlooked a grassy expanse beside the main trail going down the mountain.

"If they come back it will probably be right through here," said the Sergeant with a broad sweep of his arm. "So stay alert and don't go to sleep on me!"

Rodebaugh took the first watch. Shortly after midnight he woke me up for my turn. I couldn't believe it! It was a darkness I had never experienced before! The world was totally black. I had heard the expression "can't see your hand in front of your face" all my life but had never experienced it until this moment. This had to be the feeling of hopelessness a blind person feels. I felt my way to the position and settled in.

About an hour into my watch I heard it.

A slight rustle in the grass.

A snapped twig.

Another rustle to the right.

Still another rustle--- to the left this time!

God it's dark!

They're coming my way! What am I going to do?

I eased the safety off my rifle. Damn, that was loud. What if they heard it? I lifted my rifle and pushed it through the darkness to my shoulder. Reaching for my other shoulder, I felt for the handle of my Bowie knife. Could I really use it on somebody?

Some more movement---closer this time.

My heart was beating so hard I could hear it. They had to be able to hear it too.

They're right on top of me. They have to know I'm here. Coming right for me. Can they see through this darkness or can they just smell my fear? What am I going to do? I have to do something. I can't just let them crawl up and kill me.

I pointed my rifle towards the movement in front of me and squeezed the trigger. The sound was deafening. The muzzle flash was so bright it blinded me further.

"Who fired that shot?" demanded Lieutenant Lugo.

"I did. I heard something."

"Don't shoot any more until you have a target, dammit! You just gave away our position, you retard!"

Great!

Here I was in total darkness and I can't shoot until I see something!?!?

I really do hope there's a body out there in the morning. There has to be! That'll be the proof I need to make them understand.

The episode was very quickly swallowed up by the darkness. There was no more movement. The darkness gradually began to dissolve. Even though the thick canopy of trees prevented me from seeing it, I was never happier for the sun to come up.

A search of the area in front of my position showed no sign of the enemy. Whatever it was I had heard had vanished without a trace.

Soon after a C-ration breakfast the tanks arrived. They were heard long before they were seen. The four tanks were soon loaded down with the weapons and ammunition collected from the camp. The rice and extra uniforms were burnt, except for what the guys kept for themselves. I had one of the black pajama-type uniforms rolled up tightly in my pack. The morning went by quickly.

After lunch we were each assigned to a tank. We climbed aboard and started the long descent down the mountain. I had never ridden on a tank before. It wasn't very comfortable and was very noisy, but it sure beat walking. The trail twisted and turned. The slope was so steep at times I was sure the tank was going to turn over and kill us all..... but it didn't.

We traveled for what seemed to be hours. The lower we got the less dense the vegetation got. By the time we got to the bottom it was mostly just elephant grass with a tree here and there. The tanks circled like an Old West wagon train. We dismounted and began to dig in for the night.

Helicopters soon arrived to remove the captured weapons and the prisoners. They also brought us hot chow-----a real treat.

The tankers pulled watch in the foxholes with us grunts that night. They were afraid of being trapped inside the tanks in case of rocket attacks. While one stayed in the tank all night in case its firepower was needed, the rest seemed more comfortable being outside exposed to everything the infantry was. This thinking was strange to us, but it meant more people to share guard with, so we embraced the idea.

MORTALITY

C Company was under attack. What had begun as a very quiet patrol had turned into a battle lasting all night. We were the nearest forces to come to their aid. Scared and confused, we began our forced march into uncertainty. For a change, Third Squad was not on point today.

The explosions somewhere at the front of the column caused all of us to hit the dirt and scramble for cover. Everybody in front of us began shooting wildly into the jungle so we joined in too. By the time I needed to reload everybody had ceased firing. The frantic scrambling and shooting was followed by a long period of silence. Waycaster, Rodebaugh, Hernandez, and I looked at each other in wonder. We stared into the seemingly impenetrable jungle on both sides of the trail. Not only were we unaware of where we were; we were hot, tired, confused, and scared. Now something had happened and we had no idea what it was. We soon found out when Sgt. Bailey approached us.

"You new meat, come carry this litter!"

We all rose up and followed him up the column to where a corpse was wrapped in a poncho. A long limb had been cut and tied at each end so when we picked it up the body was suspended like a hammock.

"What the Hell is that?" Proclaimed Waycaster, verbalizing what we were all thinking.

"Guimond bought it and we have to carry him to a landing zone up ahead".

"Who's Guimond?"

"He's the new guy who came in yesterday. He was walking flank.

We got ambushed by an enemy litter carrier. He must have seen us first and decided to get in a few shots before he took off. He got Guimond here in the neck and shot up the radio while it was still on Johnson's back!"

I knew who Art Johnson was. He and Chuck Clendenon had come to A Company shortly after I did, and Johnson was assigned to carry the radio. He was called the RTO, or Radio-Telegraph operator. The whip antenna flopping behind his head, and the constant squawk of the radio, made him an easy target for the enemy to pick out.

As for Guimond, none of us knew him. New replacements were coming in daily. None of us had even seen this guy before. Now we had to get acquainted with his lifeless body as we carried it through the jungle. The tropic heat was already causing the smell of death to surround the poncho.

"Just pick him up; we've got to get moving".

The branch bent almost to the point of breaking as Rodebaugh and I lifted him on our shoulders. His body swayed back and forth as we walked, causing the strain on our shoulders to be that much more painful as we struggled along the already difficult terrain. I was in the rear, and couldn't take my eyes off the body swinging between us. Who was this guy?

Probably a month ago he was having the time of his life at home on leave. He was just another young grunt like the rest of us. And now ---just like that—he is reduced to nothing, just another dead soldier. It wasn't until that very moment I truly realized my own mortality. This could just as easily be me wrapped up in a poncho and being carried around like just so much cargo, sloshing in my own body fluids. Until now, death was just something that happened to somebody else.

Until now, this had been all fun and games! But this was real-as real as it gets. No longer could I honestly believe that we were all young immortals. Suddenly, I was vulnerable to Death at any moment, and everything was totally out of my control. All my false bravado and cocky confidence was replaced with almost uncontrollable fear.

The poncho came unwrapped from Guimond's head and for a moment I was looking deep into his eyes. What I saw was the very same disbelief in his own death that I was personally struggling with inside myself! I had never been this close to a dead person before outside of a funeral parlor. This was too real. Suddenly my stomach got queasy and my knees got weak.

"I've gotta have a break."

We came to a halt and lowered him to the ground. Waycaster wrapped the poncho back and secured it before he and Hernandez took a turn at carrying as we continued to the landing zone.

Suddenly we came to another abrupt halt. There was another period of furious activity at the front of the column, but there was no shooting this time. None of us knew why we had stopped but we took advantage of it to rest a few minutes. Sergeant Bailey approached us again. This time he was leading a shaken young NVA soldier! The enemy had his hands bound behind his back and was being led around by a rope around his waist.

"You need to keep this one with you, too. The guy on point, Naputi, had spotted him coming up the trail. Naputi hid behind a big rock and smacked him upside the head when he came by. Keep a close eye on him. We don't want to lose him. He's scared enough to do some talking."

Juan Naputi was one of the original members of the Company. He was the only person I had ever met from Guam. He was a big guy, and he had a quiet confidence that made me feel comfortable just being around him. I wish I could have seen him ambush this unsuspecting NVA soldier!

Having the prisoner in tow was a welcomed distraction to us as we moved out again.

I took the rope and walked beside Rodebaugh and Hernandez, who were now taking a turn carrying Guimond. Waycaster followed closely behind the prisoner.

We hadn't gone very far when I felt a sharp tug on the rope! I spun around, fearing that the prisoner was trying to get away. Instead of running, the prisoner was falling to the ground with Waycaster on top of him. Waycaster was beating the prisoner in the face, chest, and stomach-----everywhere he could find an opening.

With a great deal of effort we finally drug Waycaster off the terrified prisoner. We had to drag him a long way from the prisoner. He continued to kick until he was out of range. I had never seen Waycaster so angry.

The column had stopped with the fracas. When the Sergeant came back to check, I'm quite sure the scene was as puzzling to him as it was to the rest of us.

I stood holding the end of the rope. The prisoner was on the ground in a fetal position, screaming and pleading in Vietnamese. Guimond lay in the middle of the trail where he had been dropped. Waycaster was now restrained by Rodebaugh and Hernandez. That didn't keep him from kicking and fighting, trying his best to get another shot at the prisoner.

"That Sumbitch was laughing! He was laughing, lookin at Guimond. Turn me loose, Dammit, turn me loose. That Sumbitch ain't a'gonna be laughin' at our boys!"

We all were about ready to turn Waycaster loose when the Lieutenant showed up. He wasn't very happy about what had just happened. "Take this squad off this detail and send them to the rear of the column," he instructed the Sergeant. "I'll deal with them later."

It didn't bother any of us to be relieved of that particular assignment. All of us, that is, except Waycaster. He fumed about the obvious disrespect the prisoner had shown Guimond.

"I'll never take another live prisoner. Ah swear it", he groused as he scuffed his boots along the trail.

And that was the end of it. He never mentioned the incident again. And none of us ever brought the subject up around him, either.

The battle was decidedly over before we could join up with C Company. A lot of trees and large boulders were interspersed throughout their position. They did control the high ground and there was an open area large enough to accommodate helicopters.

The burnt out shell of a helicopter was wedged between two trees at the far side of the field. It had been attempting to evacuate the wounded when the enemy shot it down. The crew and three wounded men died as a result of the crash.

Dead North Vietnamese soldiers were stacked in piles just outside the perimeter. The official count was nineteen but several more had been dragged off during the night.

Since C Company hadn't had any rest for a day and a half we set up our perimeter directly in front of theirs. They could now get some sleep but still be available if we needed them. As we dug in, Art Johnson added one more body to the count. While attempting to dig a hole he uncovered a shallow grave. He moved over a few feet and continued to dig.

"Guess I'm sleeping with the dead tonight!"

I suspected that we would all be sleeping with the dead for a very long time.

Photo by permission of Art Johnson

Art Johnson

During the next few weeks the area of operations was expanded to the North. The "checkerboard" concept was adopted for this new area as well. We were lifted by helicopter into this new area of operation and conducted searching and patrolling operations.

During the last two weeks of October the Battalion had several contacts ranging from light to moderate with various size enemy units. The kill ratio was 1:8, or 54 friendly killed versus 464 enemies killed. These were the numbers on the official report. This kill ratio must have impressed somebody. All it meant to those of us doing the fighting was that fifty-four of our buddies were now dead. It also underscored the possibility that any one of us could be next.

HAPPY NEW YEAR

Here it is January and I'm half way through my tour. Will I make it? I hope so. When I think of January I still think in Central Illinois terms—namely---miserably cold. It is always blistering hot and humid here in Viet Nam. I stay wet. Even changing clothes doesn't make much difference. Five minutes after putting on dry clothes I'm soaked by perspiration again.

My poor feet are really being abused in these conditions. They stay wet and dirty—not a good combination. I hardly ever take my boots off while in the field, never knowing when I might have to scramble to safety. My calluses grow larger every day. I now have them on both the tops as well as the bottoms of my feet. The ones on the bottoms are large and layered, much like the mushrooms that grow on the sides of trees. The constant moisture keeps them soft and white. The bottoms have become as tough as the soles of my boots. Even the tops of my toes have calluses! On the tops of my feet the calluses are dark and crisscrossed, imitating the pattern of my boot laces. Around the tops of my boots are dark rings. These were caused by the many places that leeches have attached themselves to me. I removed them by holding a lit cigarette close to them until they release their grip.

A lot of physical changes have happened to me since that first day I stepped off that airplane into this suffocating heat. I thought I was in great shape when I arrived, but I was soft by comparison. There is no longer an ounce of unnecessary fat on my body. My strength and endurance have improved so much that I can now spend all day traveling through this natural obstacle course carrying a full pack.

Although I still sweat, I can now go longer periods of time without a drink of water.

The huge calluses on my feet are so tough I probably don't need boots any more. When I step on something, I can feel the pressure of it enough to tell that it is there, but I don't feel any pain. My heart is becoming the same way. That's the way calluses develop, I guess. Our bodies naturally toughen spots that are constantly exposed to damage. My emotions have been subjected to so much in the last six months that I am having trouble feeling anything inside me. It isn't that I don't care any more. Things still affect me in a negative way but it is more like acknowledging them than feeling them.

Frank Gabelman, the new guy, is taking pictures again. None of the rest of us even thought of bringing a camera when we were preparing to come to Viet Nam. But Frank did. In addition to being taller than the rest of us, Gabelman really stands out with his red hair and glasses. He was assigned to be RTO as soon as he arrived and fits nicely into that role. None of the rest of us really would want to hump that radio all day, not to mention being a prime target of any sniper who might want to take out an essential link in our organization.

The RTO is a great person to know. Not only is he "in the know" about what is going on---he is the guardian of the plastic bag that replacement batteries come in.

When reduced to a life where money has no value since there is nowhere to spend it, other items become valuable. Money can be accumulated and put in the bank and be of some use later, assuming there is a later. Immediate needs are much more important. Batteries for the radio arrived in a heavy duty plastic bag, perfect for providing protection against the elements for valuables. Pictures, letters from home, identification cards--- all these soon become papier- mache` if not somehow protected. When Frank was able to get one for me it was better than any birthday present I had ever received.

We finally got off the Operation Paul Revere kick and are now on Operation Sam Houston. All the original guys who had come over from Hawaii when the Division was deployed have spent their tour and gone home. Even though I never really connected and bonded with them, I really do miss them.

All of the Sergeants except Sergeant Rodriquez and Jimmy Hill are gone. Sergeant Rodriquez has replaced Sergeant Rivera as Platoon Sergeant. Having Sergeant Rodriquez as the Platoon Sergeant is very different. The first day he took over the Platoon Sergeant position from Sergeant Rivera he assigned me to walk point through a heavily booby trapped area. I wanted to believe that he was counting on my experience to keep us out of trouble. That's what I kept telling myself, anyway. I felt better about it when I noticed that Jimmy Hill, a Staff Sergeant, was walking flank. When we saw each other, Jimmy grinned at me and quipped,"What are you looking at, Gay Boy? Just call me a black Daniel Boone!"

I had been promoted to Specialist Fourth Class with the Military Occupational Specialty 11B30. Does that sound impressive? I was, by this definition, not only able to perform the functions of an infantry soldier but was considered able and qualified to lead a small team of three to four other soldiers. The truth was that I had just been in the Army longer than the rest of the squad. In addition, nobody else wanted the position. Since I now outranked everybody else, I was assigned as the official squad leader, a position normally filled by a Sergeant.

Fortunately for me, I had a great Platoon Leader. Lieutenant Putnam had come to Third Platoon. He seemed to accept my lack of experience while he quietly trained me in my new job.

Photo by Permission of David Dunn

Lieutenant Steve Putnam

We also had a new Company Commander. Captain Murray, who had been Company Commander since just before I arrived, was one of those rotating out. The new Company Commander was Captain Barcena. He was a Cuban who had gotten his commission somehow in connection with the ill-fated Bay of Pigs Invasion.

As part of this change in command we took part in something never heard of before in A Company—a formal ceremony in the field. For the past six months all our military formations had been purely tactical.

When we received the command"Sling Arms" I had a problem. I had long ago discarded my sling. This was how I first met our new First Sergeant, Sergeant Huley. He had noticed me fumbling with my rifle in formation and confronted me later about not having a sling for it.

"How old are you, soldier?"

"Nineteen, First Sergeant."

"I can't believe they're making snotty nosed kids like you NCOs. And where is your rifle sling?"

"I don't have one, First Sergeant."

"The next time I see you there had better have a sling for that rifle. How in the world are you going to salute an officer if you can't sling arms?"

I agreed with him that I couldn't very well salute properly and went on my way. Maybe it wouldn't be long before he would be told that most officers in the field did not want to be saluted. They disliked being identified to a sniper looking for just such a target. As for the rifle sling, a quick look around would reveal that none of us had rifle slings. Not only did the slings hang up on everything while moving through the jungle, they made a lot of noise. We had all discarded our slings long ago and taped the clips to the stock. Since we all carried our rifles at the ready to fire, a sling was just extra weight. To stay out of trouble with the First Sergeant I did get a sling which I kept rolled up in my pack when out in the field.

A Company had been picked to be "Palace Guards". This sounds a lot more impressive than it really is. A large landing zone is established and set up as a field headquarters for Battalion operations. It normally includes an artillery detachment, some heavy mortars, and a command center with lots of radios with people directing operations. The Companies took turns providing security. While all the other Companies were out in the jungle in search of the enemy, the Palace Guards enjoyed the relative security and comfort of a rear area. Short patrols and three hot meals a day were considered special luxuries.

Enjoying Palace Guard Duty

I'm now considered one of the old-timers. New guys are coming in about every day. We're able to spend some time maintaining our weapons and getting to know each other better. Waycaster, Rodebaugh, and a new guy are sharing a position. The new guy is "Happy" Howard. Happy is an inner city guy from Detroit. He was trying to act as if he was fearless, but his body language gave him away.

"Hey Happy, You skeered?" quizzed Waycaster.

We all turned to look at Howard. The question had come out of nowhere. Everybody was waiting to hear what the new guy had to say in response. He gave a long pause as he looked from man to man, trying to figure out the proper answer.

"Scared? No, I'm not scared at all!"

"Well, you're the only one here that ain't then."

Surprised and relieved at the same time, a broad smile came across his face.

"Hell yeah, I'm scared!"

As acting squad leader I've been called to the command post and given my assignment for the day. Lieutenant Putnam has a map open on a stack of C-rations for us to look at.

"The ARVN Radio Station was attacked last night. You probably heard our mortars firing in support." Pointing first to the radio station and then to an area where the mortars had been aimed he continued. "We're running some patrols, and I want you to search this area and see if we hit anybody."

I had heard the mortars firing in the night, but I didn't think anything about it because they fired every night. "H and I" fire they called it. Harassment and Interdiction. The idea was to fire at random times and locations just in case the enemy was on the move hoping to make life tough on them. As far as I know the only ones who got harassed were us poor grunts trying to get a little sleep. But it must have been effective, or they wouldn't have continued doing it.

The area I was to patrol was not very far away. I returned to my squad and we prepared to leave. We stripped down our gear and were on our way in just a few minutes.

A search like this is usually uneventful. If we had hit any of the enemy with the mortar fire, the rest of their unit would have removed any dead or wounded, leaving no sign. This time things were a little different. Reaching the location where the mortar rounds hit, I noticed a dark discoloration on a nearby bush.

When I touched the spot, it stuck to my fingertip. Blood! And not just on that bush, but scattered all over the place. Somebody got hurt very badly. A trail of the dark stain led away from the area, heading uphill and away from our camp. After making a preliminary report over the radio, we began following the blood trail.

At first the trail was very obvious to me. As it went on, however, the spots became further and further apart. A spot on the ground here. A spot on a limb there. We picked our way slowly along the trail.

"What's he following?" remarked one of the new guys.

"I dunno," remarked another.

Six months ago I would have had the same thoughts but now the signs were obvious to me. I guess by now anything out of the ordinary caught my attention. Something as simple as a straight line was cause for alarm. There are no perfectly straight lines in nature.

This was one of the many changes I had gone through without

really noticing. The jungle had been a totally foreign environment when I first arrived. Since everything was different to me at that time, everything seemed to be out of place. I am now at home here.

The signs gradually got further and further apart until I could no longer find any trace of the wounded enemy. We were about to go over a ridge that would put us out of sight of the camp. In addition, I finally realized we were traveling with nobody on point.

Discretion being the better part of valor, we returned to camp.

When I located the Lieutenant at the command post, he was in the company of Captain Barcena and a couple other officers I had never seen before. Since I avoided going around the headquarters area, there were probably a lot of officers I never knew.

Together we examined the map that was still spread out on the stack of C-ration boxes. The officers all seemed a lot more interested in my discovery than I was, but I patiently answered all their questions until they seemed satisfied. I left with the feeling that they expected me to be able to tell them more, but that's all I had for them. I was more than happy to be dismissed back to my Squad.

We beat the bush for the next two months with little or no contact. Maybe we'd get a couple of shots fired at us and we would spray the jungle, often calling in air strikes and artillery. We heard rumors of as many as two enemy battalions in the area. But we couldn't find them. We could find where they had been. A bunker complex here and there; a large group of enemy spotted along Highway 19, stores of rice and salt. We even found two US 20 MM cannons---the type usually mounted on aircraft----but no enemy of any consequence!

But we didn't need Intelligence to tell us they were there. Everywhere we went---everything we did—we had that eerie feeling of being watched. That feeling that something very dark and nasty was stalking us was ever present. Instead of getting lax and sloppy as the days of minimal contact dragged on, we just got more and more vigilant and edgy. Our caution would prove to be a good thing later.

The first week of February I got an unexpected break from the field. I was sent back to Pleiku to go to Fourth Division's NCO School. Just a month before I had been sent to the 25th Division NCO School, so this came as a pleasant surprise. Any opportunity for a break from the field was a treat to me. It was a good school, and I learned a lot about being an NCO. Since I was already doing the job, it was good to know something about how to properly perform the duties.

There was another, unexpected surprise involved in it all---I was named Honor Graduate! I wasn't any smarter or skilled than the other candidates. In fact, I really felt inferior to most of them, but I was honored.

One of the candidates was Sergeant Peterson, a squad leader from C Company. Peterson was everything I always envied---blond, strong, agile, smart, and personable. Like a lot of the others, he was a draftee. And like a lot of the others, he didn't plan to make a career of the Army like I did.

Something I did must have impressed somebody, however. The biggest surprise was that the honor was accompanied by a promotion to Sergeant E-5 11B40! Two months ago I was a Private First Class! And even though I was doing the job of a Sergeant E-6, I kept my mouth shut.

After finishing school, I spent a couple days in base camp. Third Platoon was operating in an area where they had no access to a landing zone, so I had to just hang around until they were able to receive helicopters. That meant three hot meals a day and sleeping on a real cot in a tent! I should have felt guilty living in comparative luxury while my comrades were roughing it—but I didn't really.

One day as I wandered back to the Company area after enjoying a fine lunch, a weapon discharged inside a tent that I was walking past. The tent belonged to our Long Range Reconnaissance Patrol, a group called LRRP for short. They sent small teams out on missions to investigate reports of enemy activity. A shotgun blast had torn a hole the size of a soccer ball in the side of the tent. I entered the tent to make sure that nobody was hurt. As I entered the tent from one end, a huge man entered from the opposite end. We both looked over the embarrassed LRRP guys who mumbled something that amounted to oops. Then we studied each other. The man was a Sergeant Major. A Sergeant Major is the highest enlisted rank in the Army. He was the only Sergeant Major I had ever seen up close, and he had the same last name as mine! We stood there grinning at each other a few seconds glancing at each others nametags. The Sergeant Major then turned to the man with the shotgun, told him to be more careful, and left the way he came in. There was nothing left for me to do but leave through the other entrance.

EARNING MY STRIPES

Coming back to the field was strange this time. I had moved up in rank to Sergeant. Although I had been acting as squad leader since the old-timers had all rotated out, I hadn't felt the weight of responsibility until I actually had the stripes on my sleeve.

I had a new Platoon Leader. Lieutenant Putnam had been promoted as Company Executive Officer while I was gone. His new duties would keep him in base camp at Pleiku. Sgt. Rodriquez had replaced Sgt. Rivera as Platoon Sergeant. A new Company Commander and First Sergeant, a bunch of new replacements---it almost felt like I had been reassigned!

The brief period of time during which supplies are delivered to forward areas is always a flurry of activity. I stepped off the helicopter and spent a few minutes unloading the containers full of hot chow that had accompanied me on my ride from the base camp at Pleiku.

To my surprise, Gabelman was among the sick heading back. The RTO was moving under his own power but he didn't look well at all. It was unusual to see him without the radio strapped to his back and a camera in his hand.

"What's the matter with you, Frank?"

"Sick. Malaria."

I had been there myself, so I understood the short response. He had probably been suffering with the symptoms for several days already. I remember that I sure didn't want to talk to anybody about anything. All he would desire at this point would be to lie down and either sleep or just die.

I stood to the side and watched the helicopters leave before reporting to my Company area.

Sgt. Rodriquez escorted me to my platoon's location to introduce me to my new Platoon Leader.

"Sgt. Gay, meet Lieutenant Karopzyc."

The Lieutenant looked up from the map he was studying and smiled.

"Pleased to meet you. Sergeant. Heard a lot about you. Glad to have you back!'

Even though he was a very young Lieutenant, he was one of those guys you liked and respected the first time you saw him.

We also had a new medic, Specialist Meade. The guy seemed to always be grinning. He had set up his "office" with the Lieutenant and radio operator. What first attracted my attention was that he had no weapon. Most medics wore a pistol, some carried a rifle. I even knew one who carried a shotgun. I told the Lieutenant that I would talk to the medic about keeping his weapon with him.

"Well, Sergeant, he doesn't have one. He's a conscientious objector."

"What!" I gasped. "What in the world is he doing out here with us?"

"He volunteered to be with a combat unit."

I couldn't believe what I had just heard. My father and uncles, who had all been in World War II, talked about conscientious objectors with distain. The men I had grown up around had all told me that a conscientious objector was just a coward hiding behind his religion to avoid military service. Now I had one right here in my Platoon! How was I going to maintain any kind of fighting spirit among my men with this influence in our midst? I decided to wait and see what happened. If it became a problem then I would have no choice but complain. Until then he was the closest thing to a medic we had.

The Lieutenant soon gathered the whole platoon together. On a pile of sandbags was a map of an area none of us had ever seen before.

"Men, this is where we are going. A large contingent of North Vietnamese Regulars has been spotted in this area. The B-52's are going to bomb the area tonight and we're going in the morning to see what kind of damage was done. I have to tell you this--- contact with the enemy is eminent."

"Eminent?" puzzled Waycaster "What's that mean?"

"That means the shit is gonna hit the fan!", mumbled Rodebaugh.

"Pack light," said the Lieutenant "and double up on ammunition. You're going to need it. We leave at 0600."

We heard the explosions of the five hundred pound bombs in the distance during the night. If I didn't know what was happening, I would have just written it off as artillery fire.

The next morning First Platoon left early. The rest of us acted as if they were the only ones going out on patrol that day. If anybody was watching the camp they might prematurely report back, not knowing that the entire Company would be out investigating the damage done by the B-52 bombers the night before. After giving First Platoon about a half hour lead, Third Platoon struck camp and headed towards the center of the bombed area. The first half-mile or so was very easy going and we made good time. Then suddenly the entire terrain changed, which was not unusual in the Central Highlands. We navigated a thirty foot deep gully. On the other side of the gully we made a sharp turn into the jungle. A well-worn trail led the way.

We all paused when the squelch broke on the radio. The word was passed up to us. Be on special alert. First Platoon is in contact. Look out for snipers. They were pinned down by automatic weapon fire and we were to maneuver left to assist them. It so happened that the trail turned to the left at that very time.

The squad slipped easily onto the trail with Waycaster on point as usual. Hernandez and I followed him closely.

Suddenly Waycaster raised his hand to signal a halt. He dropped to one knee and pointed down the trail. Hernandez and I quickly and quietly moved up, taking position on either side of him. Seven North Vietnamese Regulars were coming up the trail directly towards us! They all had their weapons slung over their shoulders and seemed in a hurry to get somewhere.

Waycaster pointed to himself and held up one finger. He pointed to Hernandez with two fingers. I got three. As we had been trained, Waycaster would shoot the first man, Hernandez the second and I was to shoot the third. With this plan we wouldn't all shoot the same enemy. Four of them fell with our initial barrage. The jungle behind them exploded with enemy fire.

We didn't know it at the time, but our under-manned Company of about 150 men had walked directly into an enemy Battalion base camp, with another Battalion coming in from behind them as reinforcements, bringing their total to about 1500! All I knew was that all Hell had exploded in my face! We had just kicked a hornet's nest, and these hornets had automatic weapons!

As we shot it out with the enemy in front of us, I heard a lot of people crashing through the jungle, moving to our left. As I loaded my third magazine of ammunition in what seemed as many seconds, I screamed the warning.

"Watch the left flank! They're trying to flank us!"

My voice came out much higher pitched that I expected, but that was the least of my concerns at the moment. I yelled out over the noise for the rest of my squad to move up on my left side. As soon as they did, gunfire erupted along the entire length of the column. The flanking movement ceased but the three of us remained under heavy fire.

Every weapon has its own sound, and the rattle of an AK- 47 right beside me changed my focus very rapidly. That's the enemy gun of choice! When I turned I saw Hernandez holding the AK-47 in his hands. A dead NVA soldier lay at his feet.

"He ran up right beside me! I grabbed his gun and shot him with his own gun!"

The firing went on for what seemed an eternity. They came at us in groups of four to seven. We were on an elevation and on a small point, so they couldn't advance on us without being exposed for about 20 yards. At this range they seemed more like targets than people. We shot them down as fast as they jumped up. I was so focused it felt like I was the only one fighting. Only when I took a quick glance to my side was I reassured that others were still with me. I was glad we took the Lieutenant's advice to carry extra ammunition. Waycaster and Hernandez had extra grenades, which proved very effective in slowing the assaults. Even though we were elevated, shrapnel and dirt flew by us every time a grenade went off. The amount of bloodshed was unbelievable. People were being killed and wounded all around me. Arms and legs got separated from bodies. One of the enemy soldiers stood up to throw a grenade back at us. I had him in my sights to shoot him before he could throw the grenade. It exploded in his hand, removing half of his arm and most of his face. I had to pause for a moment in disbelief of what I had just seen. The shooting from our front soon brought me back in focus.

A grenade launcher mounted below my M-16 which brought extra firepower to the fight. I was firing into the trees, causing the grenades to explode high and rain shrapnel down on the enemy. They didn't seem to like that very much. Every time I fired, I received an even heavier concentration of small arms fire in return. The amount of firing was so intense that I watched a small tree to my right erode away piece by piece. Bullets hit in front of me, beside me and sailed over my head. Rocks and splinters of trees pelted me and stung my whole body. I just knew that the next one would hit me. My body tensed in anticipation. I fired two more rounds from the grenade launcher with the same results. I heard a lot of people scattering left and right and after the fourth round the return fire lightened considerably. That was good, because I was now out of rounds for the grenade launcher. In a way, it was a relief to run out of rounds for the grenade launcher because of the amount of attention I got in return from the enemy.

The noise of battle denies description! Often times it was not even possible for the person lying next to me to hear what I was saying. Artillery and mortar rounds exploded in front of us, often sending dirt, debris, and shrapnel pouring down on us. Small arms fire rattled from both sides of the engagement. Hand grenades went off at close range. Men shouted both in command and pain. The noise became a part of my very existence. It entered my body and attacked the system almost like an electrical shock that wouldn't cease. I wanted to bury my head in the ground to escape it.

It never seemed to end. Three times we ended in hand-to-hand and bayonet fighting because we simply couldn't reload fast enough. On one assault, my rifle jammed with an enemy ten feet in front of me, his bayonet fixed and bearing down hard. I don't know why he didn't just shoot me. He charged me intent on sticking me with his bayonet. I pulled out my knife. When he lunged I brought the knife down hard between his neck and shoulder. Blood gushed straight up into my face while gurgling noises came from his neck. He went limp and fell on top of me. I pushed him off and crawled over to the place where I had been able to scoop out a shallow trench. I wiped the blood off my face and glasses as much as I could with my sleeve and cleared my jammed weapon. There was a lot of blood on my right arm. Several times I tried to wipe it off with no success.

I was bleeding!

He hadn't completely missed me with his bayonet thrust. It was more of a tear than a cut, about two inches long on my right forearm. I took my olive drab bandana from my neck and quickly folded it into a long strip. The sweat and dirt caused the wound to sting and burn as I wrapped the bandana tightly around my arm. Blood soaked and stained the bandage. After a few minutes the bleeding had stopped.

The fight moved up and down our left flank as if they were trying to find a weak spot. Just as soon as we decided they had given up on us, here they came again. After about six hours we noticed a lull to our front. Suddenly another war broke out about a quarter mile to my right. I didn't know it but C Company was advancing from that direction. The enemy had left enough troops to keep us occupied and turned their attention to C Company. The three of us took advantage of the moment to retreat and join the rest of the Platoon. We were surprised to find that they had fallen back and were occupying some enemy bunkers to our rear. We had been left out there on our own!

Meade, the new medic called me to his side as I returned. He had gathered all the wounded in a tight circle. Any doubts I may have had about this man's courage were dismissed. Even though we were still under fire Meade was moving from man to man doing all he could with limited resources. The bullets that popped and whizzed by his head didn't seem to concern him at all. He had built a make-shift shelter from logs and rocks. The young Lieutenant, who hadn't been with the Platoon more than two weeks, was fatally wounded in the chest. The Lieutenant had plugged the bullet hole with his own finger. By the time I arrived, the finger was neatly bandaged permanently in place. If the chest wound weren't enough, he also had numerous shrapnel wounds. When an enemy grenade had fallen in the middle of the wounded the Lieutenant had covered it as well as he could with his helmet. This action saved many of the wounded as well as the medic from being killed or being further wounded. The only person injured was the Lieutenant himself.

"We're out of water", said Meade.

The fact was we were all out of water. The Lieutenant had a small flask of whiskey he wanted to drink.

"Don't you have something, anything else we can give him?"

I knew that Meade really didn't approve of alcohol under any circumstances. And alcohol probably wasn't the best thing for the Lieutenant anyway. It wasn't until that moment that I remembered the can of Crème soda in my pack. Nobody had wanted it. I had put it in there because I didn't want it to go to waste.

I removed my web gear for the first time since the battle had begun. As I began to dig through my pack, I noticed the holes. Three bullets had passed completely through my pack, two from the left side and one from the front. I knew the enemy fire had gotten close at times, but I didn't realize how close until I found those holes! Miraculously, the can of soda was still intact. I handed it to Meade, who opened it and began giving the Lieutenant small sips at a time.

"Sergeant, you are a life saver," smiled the Lieutenant between drinks.

Minutes later, he was dead.

Among the wounded lying on the ground around the Lieutenant was a soldier who, until recently, had been a cook's helper. Why he was in the field was anybody's guess.

A bullet had shattered the pistol grip on his M-16 and cut his hand. He had screamed in pain while the enemy approached his position. Frozen with fear and pain, he didn't fire at all. This was when the enemy had gotten close enough to throw the hand grenade among the wounded. Luckily, another soldier noticed the situation and stopped the advance. Other soldiers moved in to fill the gap.

As I left the Lieutenant's side, the soldier with the wounded hand announced that he was also thirsty and demanded a soda from me. Pretending not to hear, I moved on.

I found the middle of the perimeter where Sergeant Rodriguez had set up his small command post. Huddled next to his radio operator, the Platoon Sergeant seemed surprised to see me.

"We've got to get these wounded out of here. I don't think the Lieutenant is going to make it."

His response was short. "I'll be glad to get us out of here if you'll secure a landing zone!"

I stood surveying the far side of the perimeter as I tried to formulate a plan. After a moment what he was telling me finally soaked in. We had no landing zone and no way of securing one. I had been so focused on my little part of the battle that I hadn't realized we were completely surrounded and cut off. We were stuck right where we were until help arrived!

Moving around the perimeter, I offered what encouragement I could and did my best to redistribute ammunition. Every once in a while a bullet would whiz by me. Sometimes they buzzed like a bee; other times they popped. By the time I heard them it was too late to do anything but move lower and pray for continued poor aim by the enemy. The bullets reminded me that we were far from being out of trouble.

The Company remained pinned down. All three Platoons were separated and unable to link up. We knew that the enemy had us greatly outnumbered. Just dumb luck had given us the advantage of surprise and allowed us to hold the high ground when the battle began. C Company was making a move through the jungle to reinforce us, but wouldn't be able to get there until the next morning.

It was now about four o'clock in the afternoon and we were running desperately low on ammunition and water. First Platoon had set up its own defensive position but weren't any better supplied than we were. Second Platoon, however, with Captain Barcena and his Headquarters Section, wasn't very far away from us and had extra ammunition.

An eight man squad was put together which quickly and easily joined up with the Second Platoon. By 4:30 the squad was ready to return to our position. They were joined by five men from the Second Platoon. The Company RTO, who had once been in the Third Platoon, insisted on joining the group, making their number fourteen.

Halfway between the two Platoons the enemy mortar rounds began raining down on the returning group. An enemy ground force, which had moved in between the patrol and Third Platoon, opened up with automatic weapons.

Pinned down by the deadly ambush, the patrol suffered heavy casualties. Eight of the fourteen were killed and the rest were now split up into two smaller groups. Unable to move in any direction, the survivors had no options other than to just hunker down and wait.

Back with my squad, the long wait also began for us. A terrible thirst began to set in. I had long ago drunk the last of the water from my canteen. Once I started thinking about being thirsty, I couldn't get it out of my mind.

Thirty feet in front of my position was a dead NVA soldier. I had been looking at him every few minutes to be sure he was really dead and not just playing possum. I had probably looked at him twenty times before I saw it. He had a canteen slung over his shoulder!

It's most likely as empty as mine, I reasoned. Maybe it's booby-trapped. I'd probably get shot before I could get it anyway. But I'm so thirsty!

"Cover me!" I told Waycaster as I crawled out to the body.

Being careful not to move any part of the body, I slipped the canteen off his shoulder and crawled back. Proud of myself for being so resourceful, I offered Waycaster a drink.

"I ain't drinkin that" he declared. "Probably full of all kinds of nasty stuff."

Great! Now I was reluctant to drink the water I had just risked my neck for. I remembered all the warnings we had been given about the hazardous of drinking untreated water. I couldn't stand it. I drank heavily from the canteen that the dead enemy soldier had placed his own lips on just hours earlier.

In the early morning hours, word was passed along the line that

C Company was very close to joining up with us, so be careful not to shoot them. When they got close enough to be heard they would blow a whistle. We would then blow a whistle in our perimeter and guide them in safely. Soon I heard a whistle blast out of the darkness to my right. My spirit soared! Finally! We were finally getting some help! My joy was short-lived, however. The jungle in front of me shrilled with whistle blasts from twenty or thirty different locations. I guess our Army wasn't the only ones that had whistles. C Company would remain where they were until daylight.

As the night wore on, B Company was helicoptered into a landing zone to our north. They began an attempt to rescue us from that direction. We could hear the heavy firing coming from their direction. The enemy had noticed them moving towards us and attacked to stop their progress. But B Company pressed on. Finally, only one sniper stood between the two Companies.

When the Captain from B Company learned about the sniper, he decided to take him out himself. He walked out toward the sniper. A squad was positioned behind the Captain with orders to fire on any muzzle flashes they saw.

As he emerged from the clearing he yelled,"Hey Charlie! Here I am! Take your best shot!"

The sniper shot the Captain and was instantly killed by the squad's fire. The Captain was wearing a vest full of magazines which saved his life. He was wounded but not seriously.

C Company arrived with the sunrise. Sergeant Peterson, who I had met in NCO school, was at the lead of C Company.

"Man, am I glad to see you guys,"

"Glad you appreciate it. I lost two of my guys back there!"

They had run into an ambush themselves and had lost several men.

By this time the enemy had disappeared into the jungle. With the area now secured, we conducted a search of the area in front of us. Dead NVA soldiers were everywhere! We knew we had done considerable damage, but had no idea how much. Altogether we had a body count of sixty-one! These were the enemies that weren't recovered when the rest retreated. There was also equipment and weapons all over the place. Everybody picked up a souvenir or two. I kept the rifle that I was almost bayoneted with and the empty enemy canteen.

During a short break I sat down next to Meade, the medic. I now had great respect for this man who I was once so skeptical about.

"You really should have a weapon if you're going to be out here with us," I began. "If you don't want to carry a rifle, I can get you a pistol."

He smiled and pulled a worn New Testament from his shirt pocket.

"No thanks. I am well armed already."

"Tell me something then---why are you out here in the field? You could easily be back in a hospital where you wouldn't get shot at."

"I'm the closest thing to a Bible most of you will ever know." I never tried to get him to carry a gun again.

A trail ran directly in front of where we had set up our defensive positions. This trail interconnected an extensive bunker system. What we had discovered was an interlocking set of base camps. A hand rail made of vines stretched along the trail which enabled the enemy to easily navigate the trail at night. That explained how they had been able to move so rapidly in flanking movements right in front of us.

Once the impromptu sweep was completed, it was time for us to leave and join the three Companies together in the area that B Company had secured. It was the best area around to land helicopters for evacuation and resupply. C Company would lead the way, and we would follow. We soon were back at the landing zone that B Company had secured.

Much to my surprise, Colonel Grainger, the Regiment Commander, was manning the position where we entered into the perimeter.

"May we join your tea party, Sir?"

"Welcome aboard, Sergeant!" was the reply.

Once all the companies were safely inside the perimeter of the LZ, hot chow was served and the wounded were tended to and evacuated. B and C Companies were to be flown out to other landing zones. A Company was to continue on foot to another location.

Making ready to depart, all unnecessary equipment was stacked in the middle of the LZ. The dead were also there. Body bags were lined up in a row. There wouldn't be room on the choppers for both the bodies and all the empty water and food containers, so the containers would have to be left behind.

"Knock holes in everything" I ordered. "Don't leave Charlie a thing he can use."

"I hope I'm not here long enough to get like you!"

I turned around to see three replacements standing there, looking in shock at the scene. It seemed that the only thing that we seasoned veterans were concerned with was making life harder for the enemy. It probably appeared to the replacements that we were unfeeling and calloused as we went about our mission while our fallen comrades were lying in body bags at our feet.

"You're just cold", muttered the replacement.

I went about my business, but couldn't stop thinking about what the soldier had said. I paused to take personal inventory. I was filthy. It had been three days since I had bathed. I still had dried blood all over my body and uniform mixed with the dirt from crawling around on the ground. A bloody bandage sagged from my forearm. The Chinese Assault Rifle with its long pointed bayonet was slung over one shoulder and the NVA canteen I had drunk so heavily from hung at my side. As I gave direction I pointed with my own rifle as if it was another finger. I knew I smelled since I had soiled my pants twice during the battle. I had to relieve myself but wasn't about to raise my body any higher than necessary. I could visualize the letter home saying:"Sergeant Gay died while exposing himself to enemy fire". I had a stubble of beard. I hadn't slept since we left on the previous day, and I must have appeared haggard. My mind and body were in full "fight or flight" mode despite being tired. I am sure that it wasn't a very good first impression for the replacements.

Had I changed? Was I really just cold? If so, would I ever be normal again? Had I left a piece of my soul in the jungle that day in March of 1967?

At the moment I had more pressing issues on my mind. I couldn't worry about what a bunch of replacements thought about me. It was now well past noon, and we had a lot of jungle to cover before dark. As I adjusted my pack and picked up my rifle, I gave the command,

" Saddle Up!"

That was when it struck me.

The pain in my gut doubled me over at first and then sent me to my knees. Then I was on my side in a fetal position. I vomited until there was nothing left, and then I vomited some more. All this was accompanied by diarrhea. Somebody had sent for a medic. He stood there for a minute watching me waste away from both ends before he kicked the enemy canteen at my side.

"Tell me you didn't drink from that!"

"I did Doc. I was just so damned thirsty."

"Well, now you know why we tell you not to, don't you?"

The Company continued on without me while I spent the next week in base camp recovering from the amoebic dysentery I had contracted from the enemy canteen. He wasn't able to kill me that day, but he sure did hurt me.

We didn't know how lucky we were that day, we seldom did. All we really knew for certain was the reality of day to day surviving. The strategy and tactics were decided somewhere far removed from where we grunts lived--- and died. The North Vietnamese we had just met were part of the NVA 66th Regiment- about 1500 men- whose mission it was to destroy us. Our undersized Company of about 150 men had been blessed with the element of surprise and the advantage of holding the high ground. We didn't know it, but we weren't done with these guys yet.

DARK DAYS

By the time I returned to duty we had a new Lieutenant. He was my fourth Platoon Leader in eight months. This one was different. Lieutenant Denino had come up the hard way. The former Sergeant had gone to Officer Candidate School to become a Lieutenant. He was a little older than most field officers, and he had a better understanding of what life as an enlisted man was like.

For the last two weeks all three companies in our Battalion had been searching for the enemy we had fought on March 12. We knew they couldn't have gone far. C Company found them. More accurately, the enemy found C Company.

On March 21, A Company left our overnight camp about 9:45 in the morning. We divided the Company up into Platoons and headed south by three separate routes. C Company left shortly after 10:00, moving to the east.

About two o'clock in the afternoon C Company found a well traveled trail. Captain Rykowski, C Company Commander sent his First and Second Platoons to search the trail in both directions. While those Platoons were searching the trail, the rest of C Company continued on their original route. After the two Platoons searched and found nothing on the trail, they began moving to the southeast.

Any time a unit was on the move, somebody was always in the lead," on point" as we called it, guiding the way. The men in the rear had the equally important task of constantly checking behind them to avoid a surprise attack from that direction.

At about 3:30 the rear security unit of the searching Platoons looked back and was surprised at what they saw. Two unarmed NVA soldiers were strolling south on the trail they had just searched! The rear element fired on the two, who quickly fled and were gone as suddenly as they had appeared.

After this bit of excitement the searching Platoons moved on again. They hadn't gone far when they discovered a bunker complex. First Platoon found a mass grave containing the bodies of nine enemy soldiers. They all began to search for more graves. The search for live enemy was briefly forgotten. Automatic weapon fire from two enemy positions brought them back to reality.

The two platoons returned fire. After a brief fight, the enemy withdrew to the southeast. One American lay wounded.

When he heard that the enemy was retreating, Captain Rykowski realized that they were running straight towards him and his unit! He radioed the two platoons that he would attack with his unit. The small, retreating enemy force was now trapped.

First and Second Platoons radioed for a medivac helicopter and settled in to wait. Nobody expected what happened next. They began receiving automatic weapon fire -from the direction the enemy had just fled! Instead of retreating, the enemy was now on the attack!

Captain Rykowski hurried his group in the direction of the new contact. This should have been his opportunity to trap the enemy between his two units. Instead, his unit was also attacked by a large enemy force. Instead of coming to the rescue, he now had problems of his own.

All attempts to move forward failed. They were pounded by enemy mortar fire. Then an enemy force of hundreds of soldiers came flooding down on Captain Rykowski's group! They wanted to kill every one of the 81 men of C Company!

As C Company battled off wave after wave of attacks, A Company was called to come to the rescue. We already knew something big was going on. We could hear the sounds of the battle three miles away. Was this what C Company had heard as they came to our rescue two weeks ago? We began forcing our way through the jungle, hoping to get there in time. The terrain was full of ravines and other obstacles, making our progress painfully slow as we moved towards the sounds of gunfire.

Most of the officers of C Company had been killed or wounded during the first ten minutes of the battle. The men beat back two human wave attacks with their own small arms before getting some much needed help from the artillery and some heavily-armed helicopters. The third enemy wave was attacking when the artillery finally got adjusted on target and stopped the attack cold. Helicopter gun ships arrived and began to systematically destroy the enemy. Each helicopter was armed with four machine guns and two rocket launchers. The enemy, faced with the deadly artillery and gunship fire, retreated towards the Cambodian border where they knew they were safe. We weren't allowed to cross that invisible line.

It was 6:30 before we could get there. We had struggled with moving through the jungle. The gunfire ebbed and flowed. It got louder the closer we got. My main concern was getting there in time. My other worry was getting shot by our own people. Neither one happened.

When the three Platoons of A Company had joined together on the way to the battle, Second Platoon had assumed the lead. As we arrived, I spotted Lieutenant Dunn, Second Platoon Leader, standing under a rock shelf talking to an officer I had never seen before. The other officer had his one arm in a sling and swung his other arm wildly as he spoke. Lieutenant Dunn motioned for Lieutenant Denino to join them and together they very shortly had a plan.

We were spread out in a long line preparing to move through the area. Hernandez was to my left. His expressionless face was difficult to read. He lit up when he smiled, but the rest of the time it was a mystery what was going on in his mind. To my right was Mike Riley, a brand new replacement. He was being initiated fast! To the right of him, Sergeant Rodriquez made the sign of the cross as we moved forward.

As we approached the battlefield, bodies were lying everywhere. Most of the bodies were lying where they had fallen, but others had managed to find some kind of shelter and tried to dress their wounds before they died. One NVA soldier, armed with a light machine gun, was lying face down with one leg cocked forward as if he had been shot down while in full stride.

"Take that weapon", said Hernandez.

Thinking it to be a good idea, I began to retrieve the gun.

"No no! The knife! Get the knife!"

I hadn't noticed the knife with a six inch blade the soldier had in a sheath on his belt. I retrieved it along with the gun.

Entering the center of the battlefield, the smell of gun smoke and fear was still heavy in the air. Small fires ignited by the many explosions still smoldered and saturated the area with misty smoke. One soldier I knew from C Company was crouched behind a gigantic anthill. The mound had to be ten feet tall and twenty feet wide. The soldier was fervently looking to his left and right and paying special attention to the top of the anthill. Scattered around him were fifteen bodies, some friend but mostly foe. The bodies were lying in such grotesque positions they may as well have been dropped from the sky and left where they fell.

"Don't go over there, Gay!" screamed the soldier. "I'm telling you, don't go there! They're over there and they're coming to get us!"

I was sure that the enemy was long gone, but I never looked on the other side of that anthill either.

We moved to the far end of the battlefield where Second Platoon was already taking position. Third Platoon settled in to their right. Although we were still receiving some sniper and occasional mortar fire, we felt comfortable moving in and attempting to take care of what was left of C Company. The survivors were moved to the center of our perimeter. Our medic was soon busy helping the other medics tend to the wounded. After they exhausted their limited supply of dressings, they requested our personal dressings. My initial thought was too keep our personal dressings for ourselves. This thing wasn't over yet, and we could need them. But we didn't need them yet, and C Company was bleeding. Most of the Third Platoon donated theirs to the cause.

Meade, the medic, was in need of a really sharp knife. He was struggling through his duties with a dull bayonet. As I passed by him, he let me know of his need.

"Hey, Sergeant Gay, I need a sharp knife. This bayonet isn't working to well for me."

He had his eyes locked on the Bowie knife taped to my web gear.

The medic was covered from head to toe with blood. He was meticulously trying to dig shrapnel out of a wounded soldier's leg with a bayonet.

Just a few days ago I would surely have been killed had I not had my knife. I didn't want to give it up, but there was a more pressing need. Then I remembered the knife I had taken off the fallen enemy soldier at Hernandez's insistence. I removed it from where I had stashed it beside my own bayonet.

When I handed Meade the knife he was very grateful.

"You always seem to show up with exactly what I need. "

Hernandez, who must have had some sort of premonition when he insisted I take it, grinned from ear to ear. I am sure the enemy soldier I took it from never intended it to be used to help save American lives. The medic grimly returned to his work, and I returned to my duties.

The scene inside the perimeter can only be described as total chaos. We were out of everything. No food, no water, no medical supplies, and worst of all, no landing zone for helicopters. A few choppers had flown over but with nowhere to land the best they could do was drop supplies through the dense tree cover. I rejoined my squad on the perimeter, and we waited for whatever would happen next.

About 500 meters from my position I suddenly heard a lone helicopter. It circled twice, hovered briefly, and was gone. I looked at my watch. It was now 7:00 at night. Somebody was out there doing something, but I had no idea what. We hadn't seen any officers lately, so we patiently held our positions.

A half hour later we heard a helicopter return to the area where the first mysterious helicopter had hovered and left. This one did the same thing. I was very puzzled by now. If we were receiving reinforcements, this was the strangest method of delivery I had ever seen. Maybe since we had no usable landing zone, troops were just being landed wherever they could.

The Radio Operator from Second Platoon called me over and cleared everything up for me.

"Have you seen Lieutenant Dunn?"

"No, I haven't seen any officers for quite awhile. What's going on?"

"Well, there's a small landing zone out there where we've been hearing helicopters coming in. First Major Crosby landed out there with about five men. They wandered around for awhile, and then the Colonel flew in and joined him. They're out there now with about nine men wanting to link up with us, but they can't seem to get ahold of anybody."

I didn't know who Major Crosby was, but we all knew who Colonel Grainger was. He was our Battalion Commander.

"Sit tight; I'll go see if I can find Lieutenant Dunn for you."

Moving towards the center of our perimeter, I passed the remnants of C Company. They were huddled in their own informal area. Hyper-vigilant, nervous, scared---I can't begin to fathom the range of emotions they had to be feeling. All but six of them had been killed or wounded. Riley and a few other guys from A Company were with them, silently providing comfort and security. I shuddered when I realized that this could easily have been the fate of our own Company just two weeks ago.

When I reached the center of the perimeter the problem became clear. A Company Command Center had been set up in an enemy bunker complex. All the officers and higher ranking NCOs were standing in a tight semi-circle. Captain Barcena paced back and forth in front of them, ranting in his broken English, but often slipping into his native Spanish. Nothing else seemed to be going on here. Leaving the chaos behind me, I realized I had to move on my own.

"I need some volunteers," I said to nobody in particular when I returned to the perimeter. "We need to go get the Colonel."

I had no sooner spoken than three riflemen and a machine-gun crew stood up.

"I'm going with you" announced one of the Second Platoon riflemen.

I hadn't even noticed him before, but now I recognized him. The last time I had seen him he was working at base camp as a supply clerk.

"What're you doing out here?"

"Hey, I'm Infantry too. I was envious of you guys going out and kicking ass while I sat up in base camp, so I requested coming out in the field. I didn't even think that we could get our asses kicked. C'mon, let's go get the Colonel while I still feel brave."

With that we were on our way through the pitch black jungle. There were sounds of movement all around us. We cautiously approached the area where only minutes ago the mystery helicopter had hovered and left. Suddenly a voice commanded from the darkness.

"Halt! Who goes there?"

"Sergeant Gay, A Company."

"Damn, am I glad to see you!"

As we entered the clearing, I saw why. The challenger was Captain Lanning, the Assistant Operations Officer. I could see four soldiers lying prone in the firing position. The lanky profile of the Colonel lingered in the background. The Captain, the Colonel, and a few riflemen and radio operators, had dropped into the clearing and secured it. If any enemy were still around, the small crew would have been easy picking.

Leaving my small team to help secure the position, I returned to the perimeter. The Colonel with his group soon joined us, and it wasn't long before some semblance of order materialized. We began to make provisions for evacuating the wounded.

By 7:00 we had begun clearing a landing zone to evacuate the wounded. The area available for evacuation was very small and would only allow for one helicopter at a time to come in and hover. The wounded would then have to be raised by a hoist, one at a time, up to the hovering helicopter. It seemed like we had the situation under control. The first medical evacuation helicopter arrived about 8:00. They hovered above our tiny landing zone and prepared to begin the extraction operation.

We had brought a large supply of C-4 plastic explosive with us, knowing that there would be no existing landing zones. The C-4 was to be used to blow down trees and open up an area. The explosives had been collected from those carrying it and stacked in one pile.

Small fires left over from the battle were still smoldering

throughout the area. The air movement created by the hovering helicopter was causing burning embers to blown dangerously close to the pile of explosives!

Lieutenant Dunn realized that a disaster was about to happen. He was frantically attempting to get the helicopter to abort its mission when the munitions exploded. The helicopter lurched violently in the air until its rotor blades struck the trees. The aircraft crashed into the middle of our small landing zone, killing two of its crew members.

Photo by permission David Dunn

Lieutenant David Dunn

Colonel Grainger had passed a better site for a landing zone before linking up with us, and we soon relocated. Once we felt secure, the medical evacuation helicopters were called to return. We now had a landing zone where they could actually land.

The first helicopter arrived about ten-thirty. The evening was going by fast. On board were the Battalion Surgeon, Captain Stilp, and a team of engineers armed with chain saws. The engineers immediately began enlarging the landing zone while the rest of us were organized into task groups----litter parties, medical teams, and security. By 1:30 in the morning, all the most seriously wounded had been evacuated and the Colonel, with his command group, were airlifted back to their headquarters at the fire base. The slightly wounded would have to wait until daylight to be evacuated.

It took three hours and fifteen sorties of helicopters to remove the thirty-four most severely wounded members of C Company. Most of the wounded left their weapons with us, so we were well armed in case of another attack. Luckily for us, this fight was over. We settled in for what was left of the night.

The jungle was never as quiet as it was that night. Usually the wind blows a little, or some animals move around. But not on that night. It was as if nothing existed beyond the perimeter of our camp. Just before sunrise a voice from the jungle broke the silence.

"Charlie Company!"

A mad shuffle ensued since everybody was now wide awake.

"Charlie Company!" he repeated.

"Who's there?"

"It's me, man. Don't shoot me man. Please don't shoot. I'm coming in."

Not knowing what to expect, every man was ready, rifles trained at the barely visible jungle. Suddenly he just appeared, seemingly out of nowhere. One lone GI, unarmed, was standing just feet away from one of our foxholes. The medics leapt up as one and ushered him in.

The C Company medic recognized him as one of their own.

"What happened to you?"

"I don't know. I just woke up and everybody was gone."

"Do those wounds hurt?"

"What wounds?"

It wasn't until he looked down did the three wounds, two in his left arm and one in his left side, begin to bleed. He immediately collapsed. The medics hurried him to their makeshift aid station where they began treating him as the radio operator called for a medivac helicopter.

The chopper soon arrived to carry the wounded, disoriented man away. Supply choppers arrived shortly afterwards bringing some much appreciated hot chow. As we ate, we all wondered how that man had survived the night. How he kept from bleeding until in our safety is one of those mysteries we'll never understand.

B Company arrived and replaced what was left of C Company. Together, we were going to make a search of the entire area to retrieve any bodies of own troops that might still be out there and get an idea how many enemy had been killed. None of us were looking forward to it. Bodies were starting to smell and there were probably enemy booby traps around. There might even be some enemy who decided to stay and fight rather than flee with the others.

After chow we began our search. Sure enough, we weren't done taking losses! One group got in a firefight with two NVA soldiers, killing them both. Five A Company guys got wounded trying to retrieve a dead GI. The body had been booby trapped using American hand grenades. One of those wounded later died.

Third Platoon was assigned to move out 200 meters to our front and then sweep left until joining First Platoon, who had moved forward 200 meters before sweeping right. When we did join them, they were standing in front of ten shallow graves. Seven of the graves were what one would expect--- five to six feet long with a mound of dirt covering a body. The difference with the other three was that the bodies were much too long for the graves. Arms and legs extended from both ends. All three were wearing American issue jungle boots.

Lieutenant Denino turned to the Third Herd.

" Dig them up."

As we uncovered the bodies we were relieved to see that they were not wearing American uniforms but the khaki uniforms of

North Vietnamese Regulars. No badges or patches were visible to distinguish what unit they had been a part of. The three were all at least six feet tall and had bandanas covering their faces.

"Uncover their faces", ordered the Lieutenant. "I have to be sure they're not some of our guys. They're just too tall to be gooks."

None of us really wanted to touch those mangled bodies, let alone look them in the eye. Finally Waycaster handed me a forked stick he got from somewhere, and I slipped the bandana from one of the corpses. An oriental face stared defiantly at us.

The First Sergeant was among those who had showed up to look at our find. "Chinese advisor, Sir," snorted the First Sergeant. "The bastards had Chinese advisors. No wonder they were able to set up such a slick ambush."

To my relief, the Lieutenant ordered us to cover them back up before they started stinking. I don't know if he had actually been satisfied or if the corpses turned his stomach as badly as they did mine. We were more than happy to put dirt on those bodies and go on our way.

By now, it was about eleven o'clock in the morning and all patrols had finished their sweeps. Lieutenant Denino radioed that we were returning to the perimeter. After a brief discussion, he handed the handset back to the radio operator.

"We're not done yet", he frowned.

I think he was as ready to return to the perimeter as the rest of us were. Even though it was pretty obvious that the enemy was long gone, there was still an ominous feeling in the air. Everybody has felt it at one time or another, that feeling that something bad was about to happen at any second.

He turned to me and asked, "Do you remember where that Medivac chopper went down last night?"

"Sort of."

I actually remembered too well. It had gone down not too far from where we were now standing.

"We have to go retrieve a body."

"Let's go, Third Herd," I said to nobody in particular.

None of us were really too excited about the prospect of dealing with more dead bodies, but we were the closest to the wreck, so off we went.

We smelled the helicopter long before we saw it. There was an odor of fried electronics mingled with aviation fuel so thick we should have been able to see it. The wreck was on its side with what was left of the propellers wedged in the ditch made by a small stream. The huge blades partially dammed the flow of water.

Waycaster climbed up the wreckage and peered inside.

"Thars one in hyar," He drawled.

"Get him out." ordered the Lieutenant.

I climbed up to help Waycaster. Inside, the young Sergeant lay on his back staring straight ahead. Once inside, we realized we had a big problem. The Sergeant was entangled in what seemed like miles of wiring one never ordinarily sees. I never imagined there were so many wires in a helicopter. And he seemed to be wrapped up in every wire there was.

"Happy" Howard, one of the new replacements, joined us. Rigor mortis had already set in, making the stocky Sergeant stiff and totally unbendable. Frozen in a spread-eagle position, he seemed to resist all our attempts to get him untangled. Howard suddenly turned pale.

"I can't deal with this".

He left a lot faster than he had entered.

"What the Hell is taking so long", demanded the Lieutenant. "You've been in there fifteen minutes. We have to get going."

We had no idea it had been so long.

"You've got to break his arm", declared Waycaster.

I knew he was right. As repulsive as the idea was, there was no other way. I put my foot on his right arm near the shoulder. Grapping his right wrist, I gave a strong, sharp tug. The arm snapped in two and flopped around in my hands like it had never been attached. I threw up in the corner of the fallen aircraft.

Waycaster and I forced the dead Sergeant outside through the door. The rest of the squad grabbed him and pulled him the rest of the way outside. Waycaster and I just stood looking at each other. What could we say? After a few seconds, we climbed out of the helicopter and joined the others.

A litter had been made by stretching ponchos on poles. Soon we were on the move back to the perimeter. I walked beside the dead Sergeant. I noticed for the first time that he was carrying a 45 Caliber pistol in a holster on his pistol belt. That was proof to me that the enemy had fled without checking on the wrecked helicopter. I removed the pistol from the holster and stuffed in my own web gear. "Sorry," I whispered to my fallen comrade. "You won't need this anymore, but I just might."

The patrol returned to the perimeter without further incident. Everybody went back to their assigned positions. Some supply choppers came with hot chow and removed the bodies, which by then had been neatly tagged and placed in body bags. Waycaster and I stood guard on the perimeter while the rest of the Third Herd went to chow. Neither of us was very hungry.

Silently, we sat in the dirt beside the machine gun. Waycaster absently whittled on a stick while I fiddled with my pistol. It was Waycaster who broke the silence. "Ah bet heeda done the same thing fer you."

We looked each other in the eyes for the first time since sitting down. I noticed for the first time that Waycaster now had that look in his eyes- that hardened look a man gets once he has stared death in the eye. Once he has that look it never goes away. I wondered if I had it too. I must if he does.

"Thanks".

I stood up, stuck the pistol in my belt, and wandered off, pretending to inspect the rest of the perimeter.

STAND DOWN

We had been in the field for six hard weeks and we were more than ready for a break. Six weeks isn't a long time for most people, but six weeks to a grunt is an eternity. Just living in the Spartan conditions is a real strain on the body, even for a nineteen-year old body. When we traveled light, everybody was still carrying more than fifty to sixty pounds of equipment. Just breathing was enough effort to cause a person to sweat in the hot, humid climate. Fighting through the jungle day after day, fueled only by the nourishment of C-ration meals, sleeping on the ground when we could sleep, and living in the constant fear and uncertainty of what was going to happen next; all these had taken their toll. We were physically and mentally worn completely out. Finding out that we were going back to the relative safety of base camp at Pleiku was Christmas, Thanksgiving, and Easter all rolled up in one package.

First order of business was a hot shower. That wouldn't sound like a big deal unless you were the person who hadn't had a hot shower in six weeks. Washing your face and crotch with cold water out of your helmet just does not substitute for a steamy, hot shower. It was the first time in a long time we actually felt clean, and clean is such a great feeling when you've been so nasty for so long.

Putting on a clean uniform with dry socks was the icing on the cake after the hot shower and shave. We didn't have to shave that often since most of us weren't that far out of puberty, but it still felt great. Shaving once a week kept the whiskers down for most of us. Clean, dry socks on freshly powdered feet was a major treat after being out in the boonies for such an extended period of time. Our feet stayed wet, not only from sweating so profusely but from wading through small streams almost daily. Nothing dried very quickly in the jungle. To make it worse, grunts rarely took their boots off in the field.

Having a hot meal served in a mess hall where a soldier could sit down in a chair at a table was also a real treat. Everybody in the Squad sitting and eating at the same time is not even possible in the field. This seems like a very small thing until a person has lived in an environment where he has to be on constant guard. Enjoying a hot meal with the people you depend on day in and day out for your very existence brings closeness unparalleled even in the closest of families. It took a couple of days for our systems to become used to real food. After surviving on C-rations for so long, mess hall food seemed a little greasy. But we did soon adapt to the change.

Many times the troops hadn't been paid for a couple of months. Not that is really an issue since there was really nowhere to spend it. Unlike other places of duty where there were clubs, movie theatres, and other places for soldiers to spend their pay, the grunts in Viet Nam had none of those luxuries. All the basic needs were taken care of for us, as basic as those were. Besides, leisure time was something that everybody else had. Money didn't really mean anything to us.

There weren't that many places to spend it and everybody was more than aware that there may not be a tomorrow for any of us. Nobody was making too many long range plans. When a card game broke out, it might remind you of the Wild West days of the movies. Guns on the table, drunken gamblers passed huge pots of money back and forth until they finally went broke or just got tired and went someplace where they could sleep it off. It really never made any difference who won since money meant much less than a clean rifle and someone you could rely on at your side.

The alcohol was usually flowing pretty well at this point. Everybody had gone to draw the beer ration. Grunts were rationed two free cans of beer a day. Of course, this beer was seldom delivered out to the field, so a rest period in base camp usually resulted in a lot of hangovers. Once the free beer was gone, there was still plenty of cash left around to continue the party. We intended this to be the party of all parties.

Rodebaugh showed up with an old guitar he got from somewhere.

We were all amazed the first time we found out he could play. It didn't take long for him to impress us with his skill. The great thing about him was that he was not offended by the musical ineptness of the rest of us. We couldn't carry a tune but we made up for it with our enthusiasm. Besides, the more we drank the better our singing became.

More often than not, Waycaster would begin wailing" The House Of The Rising Sun" and the whole Third Herd would join in. "House", as we referred to it was our unofficial theme song. I don't know how or when it was adopted. The song just seemed to fit. Many of the men had taken Advanced Infantry Training at Fort Polk in Louisiana and had fond memories of New Orleans. Maybe there really was such a place. I never heard of it before and if any of the others knew of such a place they weren't talking. "There is a House in New Orleans, they call The Rising Sun, and it's been the ruin of many a poor boy, and Lord I know I'm one." It seemed that everybody knew that chorus, since after a while and several beers; the chorus was all we sang.

We had a chance to catch up on our mail, go to town, take care of administrative matters, and relax for a few days. Of course it wasn't all fun and games. There was still guard duty, mess duty, beautifying the company area, and all those other types of busy work the Army can't seem to function without. But it was a much more comfortable, relaxed life than living in the field. It certainly felt safer. When we learned that we were going back out, I secretly wished I had been assigned to Headquarters Company as a clerk typist after all. Wishing didn't make it happen, and by now I had such a strong bond with my brothers in A Company, I couldn't imagine being safe while they were in harms way.

My mail had backed up. I always enjoyed mail call, especially at times like this when I could read and savor it all at a leisurely pace. Although I loved getting mail from family, I looked forward to my letters from Dee. Dolores Elizabeth Ann Cornelius. I had never actually met Dee but I felt like I'd known her all my life. While in the hospital recovering from malaria, some Red Cross folks had come through the ward to visit. They had enlisted girls from across the

States willing to write to soldiers. I gave the Red Cross people my address and very soon I got my first letter from the Queens in New York. Ever since then, without fail, I got a letter from Dee every week. A lot of guys with steady girlfriends back home didn't do that well.

When I opened the letter, a newspaper clipping was inside. It was an obituary for Jim Perrone who had been killed in the battle on March 12. Perrone was in the Second Platoon but everybody knew him and liked him. I especially liked the way he seemed to be able to find the humorous side to even the worst situations.

As I was reading it, Jimmy Hill walked by outside my squad tent and got involved in a conversation with some other guys outside. I knew that Jimmy and Perrone had been close friends. They were both from New York City, and both had a great sense of humor.

I raised my voice enough to be heard through the mosquito netting that served as a tent wall. "Hey, Jimmy, Let me talk to you when you're done there."

After a couple minutes Jimmy came in the tent. "What's up?"

"I thought you'd be interested in reading this."

Handing him the clipping, I went back to reading my mail.

It took only a second for him to scan the clipping. To my surprise, he angrily threw it to the floor.

"Man, what the Hell is the matter with you? You should have warned me about what that was!"

Taken aback, I uttered, "I'm really sorry. I thought you'd want to see it."

"Well, you could give a guy some warning," He stormed out of the tent, wiping his tears with the hand away from me so I couldn't see.

As I watched him slowly move away, I was taken by how much A Company had changed in the past nine months. Hill, Hernandez, Waycaster, and I had been the new guys. Art Johnson and Chuck Clendenon had come shortly after us. Now we were the old-timers. Frank Gabelman had come just after the start of the year. Mike Riley had arrived about the middle of this month. Tom Gardner and Roger Bolerjack had come in together just a week ago. Every day there were new faces around the Company. Would they make it through their tours? Would I? One thing was certain---none of us would return as the same person.

The Chaplain, Sgt. Rodriquez, and the Lieutenant have their heads together. I thought it curious that our Chaplain carried an Army 45 pistol on the few occasions I saw him out in the field. When I asked him about it he kind of wavered.

"Well, as you probably know, I fly in helicopters a lot. I carry the pistol for protection from wild animals in case we crash in the jungle."

That reasoning would have been good enough for me if we didn't have a medic with us who went everywhere we went ---unarmed.

After awhile they called us NCOs together.

"Tomorrow we are going to hold a memorial service for our recent KIAs. We'll form up at 0800 to march to the chapel", announced Sgt. Rodriquez.

"No we won't!" announced Jimmy Hill.

How out of character was that! Jimmy was a good soldier. Never before had I seen him balk for even a second at any order. Yet there he stood, glaring defiantly at the Platoon Leader and the senior NCO.

"What?" retorted Lieutenant Denino.

"With all due respect, Sir, we don't march to church."

The next morning the Third Platoon walked to the Chapel together. It was a wonderful, moving service. Many sincere words were spoken in honor of our dead. When it was all over, we returned to the Company area and continued to mourn, each of us in his own way.

After a few days of rest we were preparing our gear to move out once more.

CARIBOU AND WATERMELON

The Fourth Infantry Division had come to Pleiku. The Fourth Division was from Fort Lewis, Washington, where they were well trained in conventional warfare. The Twenty-Fifth Infantry Division, on the other hand, came from Hawaii, and every man was trained as a Jungle Warfare Expert. We believed that the guys from the Fourth Division had a lot to learn in a hurry.

There was now an entire Division doing what we had done with only a Brigade. The way the boys from the Fourth Division acted, an outside observer would believe they were solely responsible for chasing the enemy away and securing the region. The truth was that they had inherited it from us, the Twenty-fifth Division. And we had inherited it from the First Cavalry Division.

We were soon to find out the rest of the story.

"I don't like it," moaned Waycaster. "No sir, I don't like it, not one little bit".

"What is it now?" groused Rodebaugh. "Seems there's always something you don't like. Me, I'm happy as hell. If the Lieutenant wants us to sit here around the Company area, I'll do that all day. It beats the hell out of beating the brush."

I silently agreed with both of them. It was well past time for us to return to the field, and sitting around the mess hall sure did beat going out into the jungle. However, the Lieutenant never got us all together just for a little chit-chat. It usually meant that something serious was about to happen, and he wanted to explain it only one time.

We all jumped to our feet at the call of "Attention," shortly followed by "At Ease".

Nobody had come to the full position of Attention; it had been so long since any of us had actually done that we would have been hard pressed to remember how.

"Take your seats, men. I have some news for you."

"I am sure that by now all of you know that the Fourth Infantry Division is now in Pleiku. What you may or may not know is that we are now under their operational command. In a few months we will become part of the Fourth Infantry Division. We also have a new assignment. You men will no longer have to beat the jungle."

We all just looked at each other. Being a part of the Twenty-Fifth was a source of pride to most of us, but not having to go back out into the jungle would be well worth any ego crash. So what was it----- they just didn't need us anymore---- or what was the deal? It all sounded too good to be true.

The Lieutenant had had his fun.

"We are being relocated. We will leave Pleiku tomorrow for a little place on the other side of the country called Duc Pho in Quang Ngai Province. That's on the other side of Da Nang from here".

It may as well have been on the other side of the world if Da Nang was supposed to be some point-of-reference for us. None of us could point to Pleiku on a map, let alone tell you where it was from Da Nang. Most of us did know that Da Nang was where some Marines were stationed. Unless we had gone to a hospital, none of us had seen a Marine since we had been in Viet Nam.

"We are going to be part of Task Force Oregon," continued the Lieutenant. "The Republic of Viet Nam wants to rebuild a highway from north to south clear across the Country. It seems every time they build a bridge, it's not long before the Viet Cong blow it up. We are going to Duc Pho, let our presence be known, and see that this road gets completed if we have to build it ourselves!"

Waycaster poked Rodebaugh in the ribs. "Hell, we oughta git them boys that keep up that Ho Chi Minh Trail over there. We bomb the shit outa them every night and thair back in business the next morning afore sunrise."

Ignoring the comment, the Lieutenant continued.

"Tomorrow morning we will fly out and set up a new base camp. All men will carry full field gear and once we are established, all remaining gear will be packed up by our Quartermasters and brought to us. Since there is no established airfield at Chu Lai, we'll be flying in on Caribou aircraft. Men, these planes are the Infantryman's best friend. They can fly in and land on a strip no bigger than a football field. Everybody get ready and we will leave after chow in the morning."

"I guess if Santy Claus kin fly around the world with some reindeer, we kin git across Viet Nam with some Carryboo, whatever they is," commented Waycaster on our way out.

The next morning we all had our first experience with Caribou aircraft. The camouflaged, twin-engine planes were sitting on the runway when our trucks arrived.

"Lookit that tail!" yelled Waycaster. "It sticks up in the air like a rooster's tail!"

The tail did stick up exceptionally high, and below it was the loading ramp.

"First thirty men, first plane," yelled the Air Force NCO directing our loading.

"Whares the seats? Thar ain't no seats in hyar!" yelled Waycaster.

He was telling the truth. We stared into the cargo hold, which was about thirty feet long and twenty feet wide, and empty.

"Sit on the floor!" yelled the NCO. "First man in sits on the floor facing the back. Next man sits between his legs, and so on all the way to the back. Make four rows. Come on, do it! We ain't got all day!"

I never would have believed that the cargo area would hold thirty men in full combat gear. But after fifteen minutes of shuffling, fussing, scooting, and grunting, here we were, crammed inside the bowels of the strangest looking aircraft any of us had ever seen, headed to who knows where. With much groaning and straining, the heavily loaded Caribou lifted off the short runway in the Central Highlands.

We had been so involved with getting situated inside the plane none of us had paid any attention to the construction of the craft itself. I believe it was Hernandez who noticed it first. I was sitting on the hard floor trying to decide which was making me more uncomfortable; my own overloaded pack which was now beginning to dig heavily into my shoulders or Waycaster's pack which was now beginning to push painfully into my crotch. Hernandez was seated beside me to the right with Rodebaugh packed tightly in his crotch. His gaze was fixed on the wall beside him. His eyes were as wide open as I had ever seen them. He made the Sign of The Cross as he appeared to be trying to crawl up under Rodebaugh's pack.

Then I noticed it myself. The body of the plane appeared to be made of canvas stretched over a pipe frame. We watched in horror as the walls expanded and contracted, much like lungs breathing. Occasionally, it would cough, making a flapping noise that soon settled back into a steady hum. I tapped Waycaster on the helmet and pointed it out to him. He would have jumped up and run, but we were packed too tightly for anybody in the middle to move, let alone stand. Where he would have run to was also a good question.

"Oh my Gawd!", he shouted. "Please git me back on the ground in one piece! Ah'd rather git shot at!"

It wasn't long after this discovery that we approached our destination. The plane was losing altitude as we felt it make a wide sweeping circle. We hit the ground hard forcing Waycaster's pack sharply into me, almost knocking the wind out of my lungs. Before we could recover from the bumpy landing, the engine propellers reversed direction, causing us to be further shaken up. Hernandez's eyes were no longer wide open. They were tightly closed and both hands were on top of his helmet as if he was trying to stuff his entire being inside.

Suddenly the plane made a sharp jerk to the right and stopped. The ramp at the rear of the plane fell open with a crash.

"Everybody out!" screamed the NCO who had loaded us. "Let's go! Move out!"

It was an order that didn't have to be repeated. We all half-staggered, half-fell out of the back of the plane.

The last man was barely out before the strange planes disappeared with a great deal of noise and dust. There we stood in a totally different world. It was still ungodly hot, but the heavy vegetation of the jungle and the rolling hills of the Central Highlands had been replaced with flat, open country punctuated with rice paddies.

We reformed the Company and began the process of establishing ourselves. Once we staked out our respective territories, we divided our time between fortifying the perimeter and patrolling our new home.

It almost felt like going on a picnic, patrolling our new home. Gone were the jungles, rolling hills, and deep ravines. Instead, we could see for miles. A false sense of security fell over all of us. We couldn't be in any danger from any enemy since there was obviously no place for them to hide. Our opening days were easy and laid back. We patrolled the same terrain over and over again, usually with the other squads in sight on both sides and to the front and rear. What a treat! We now had it made! We were all going to just stroll our way through the rest of our tours.

On the second day we were patrolling along some rice paddies. Another Platoon from our Company had just passed through this same area an hour ago. Rodebaugh and Hernandez were on point that day. Even though we were extremely comfortable, we were still taking precautions. Soon it became necessary to cross a rice paddy. I sent the point team across first. Once across, they would take up protective firing positions to cover for the rest of us to cross. In case of an ambush we certainly didn't want to have the entire Platoon out in the open.

While the point team was making their way across the rice paddy, I stepped over to where Hazelwood had found some shade close to a small hut. As we enjoyed a quick smoke, a young boy came out of the shack. We looked at the lad in utter disbelief. Cradled in his arms was a twenty-pound watermelon! The first watermelon either of us had seen since we had arrived in Viet Nam!

"Hey GI, you buy melon? Number one! Only twenty P. You want?"

I couldn't believe it. A real watermelon! And I could have it for only twenty cents.

"If you don't git it, I am," stated Waycaster.

I was grinning from ear to ear as I dug into my pocket and fished out the soggy piece of paper that had come to represent real money for us. Twenty cents for the treat of the year? Of course!

The point team had made their way across the rice paddy by now and was signaling for the rest of us to cross. Watermelon under one arm, rifle cradled in the other, and with a big silly grin on my face I strolled out into the middle of the rice paddy with the rest of the patrol.

Then the shot rang out.

Sniper!

Dropping the watermelon in the water, I scrambled to the far side of the rice paddy with everybody else, seeking protection behind the nearest wall of the paddy. One shot was all there was. No sniper was in sight. Everybody studied the terrain in front and to both sides in search of the unseen enemy.

Suddenly Waycaster began laughing. He was looking behind us as the lad who sold me the watermelon disappeared into the stand of timber on the other side of the rice paddy. Clutched in his arms was my watermelon.

"I thought it were a damned good price fer that melon," laughed Waycaster. "I wonder how many times he's sold that same melon today."

During conversations with guys from other platoons I found out that I was at least the third victim of the enterprising lad that day. We had many a laugh over that watermelon later. At the time, however, it was anything but funny. I don't know who would have had to tell my family I had been killed over a watermelon. I am glad nobody had to. I sure wasn't going after it because somebody was still out there with a gun somewhere. The melon was probably waterlogged by this time anyway.

Any time an infantry unit stayed put in one location in Viet Nam for any length of time; a small village of makeshift huts soon sprang up nearby. Duc Pho proved to be no exception. These little villages were similar to the old west boom towns, with residents offering every service imaginable. They were also full of beggars, con men, and thieves.

Since there were no permanent buildings at this time, a lot of supplies were simply stacked neatly just inside the perimeter. One day, when we were particularly bored, Waycaster appeared with a case of C-rations. It took a great deal of patience, but he managed to slip the bands off the carton without cutting them. He then removed the contents of one box and carefully placed a smoke grenade inside. He pulled the pin, holding it inside the box in such a manner that the lever couldn't fly off. We all watched in silence as he replaced the box back in the carton and deftly slid the bands back on the case.

"Watch this, Y'all!" he beamed as he placed the doctored case on top of a stack of C-rations close to the perimeter. "I'm gonna catch me a rat!"

It wasn't very long before we saw a kid sneaking up to the perimeter. He couldn't have been more that 11 or 12 years old. After looking left and right several times, he grabbed our case of C-rations and ran as hard as he could. The box was almost as big as he was. We watched him until he disappeared into one of the makeshift huts.

A few minutes later a great commotion arose from inside the hut. A bunch of hollering was shortly accompanied by red smoke pouring through every opening and crack in the hut. The lad came running out of the door just as fast as his little legs could carry him. A woman, presumably his mother, was close on his tail smacking him about every third step with a broom. It was one of those times when it would have been a real treat to understand the Vietnamese language.

DIFFERENT PLACE-DIFFERENT WAR

It didn't take very long for Task Force Oregon to get organized. The three Companies of our Regiment were teamed up with the Blue Team of B Troop from the First Cavalry Division. A "Team" in the First Cavalry Division was a Company of infantry with at least two helicopter gun ships with them at all times. In the past, helicopters had just transported us someplace and left. Now when we went into action, we had heavily armed helicopters flying on either side of us all the time. There were also smaller observation helicopters in the air keeping everybody informed of the enemy's movements. What a change this was for us. In the jungle we were fortunate if we knew what was thirty feet in front of us! Air support didn't usually arrive until after the fighting was over. Now we almost had eye contact with them all day!

A year before the 25th Division came to Viet Nam, the First Cavalry Division had operated in the same Central Highlands region that our Brigade just left. They had been the first American Division to fully engage the North Vietnamese Army in battle. They fought the very same tough Regiments we had tangled with in March. We felt really comfortable about having this history in common. Of course, we did have to tell them that they had left more than a few of the enemy for us to deal with.

We moved from Duc Pho to establish LZ Montezuma as a base of operations. Our support included the Air Force, two artillery batteries, and the Red Team and the White Team of the 1st Squadron, 9th Cavalry. We could also count on Navy destroyers for fire support. Thus organized, we began Operation LeJeune.

LZ Montezuma

I was beginning to believe that those Caribou aircraft had dumped me into a completely different war. This new terrain was totally foreign to me. I had become at ease in the jungle. Now the learning process had to begin all over again. Even the air had a different feel and smell to it.

The enemy was also different. Just as dangerous, but different. We had not fought battles with Viet Cong units in the Highlands. The Viet Cong were civilian soldiers. In the Highlands they served mostly as spies, scouts, and supply personnel for North Vietnamese Army units. The North Vietnamese were well trained and equipped. Their tactics were similar to our own. They wore khaki uniforms and helmets. Once ready to fight they would stand their ground valiantly. We knew who they were as soon as we saw them.

The Viet Cong were not as easy to recognize. They might be that friendly barber who shaved your face with a straight razor yesterday. Maybe it was that farmer peacefully tending his rice paddy or that woman washing her laundry in that stream near camp. Any or all of them could don a uniform that resembled black pajamas tonight and try to kill you. Some Viet Cong units did form and act like regular army units. These small units usually included members of the North Vietnamese Army.

The other big change was our method of operation. Enemy units couldn't hide here as well as they could in the jungle. When they were spotted we moved quickly with a lot of air and artillery support. In the jungle the fight was almost over before any support could arrive. Here the support elements were an ever present part of the operation.

Another big change was in my personal attitude. I was a different person altogether. Who was this hard case who now wore my uniform and answered to my name? And why had I come to hate anybody who even looked oriental? Not only was I one of the old guys but was daily becoming a short-timer. Nine months had seemed likes a lifetime. Sometimes I had difficulty remembering any other life. Could I survive another three months? Everybody seemed to be bonding well, but there was still a distance between me and the rest of the guys. I was now acting Platoon Sergeant which further widened the gap.

A Company had been designated as Palace Guards. We stood by in reserve at LZ Montezuma to serve as reinforcements. All of the other Companies were assigned areas to search. The Blue team was conducting search and destroy operations in the northeast area of our operations where a Company of 50 to 75 Viet Cong and North Vietnamese Army soldiers was suspected to be located.

On the 16th of April, Blue Team left LZ Montezuma early in the morning. They captured a suspected Viet Cong outside the village of Thach Thang. The prisoner told them that 61 North Vietnamese Army and Viet Cong soldiers had stayed in his town the previous night. While searching the area, Blue Team made contact with some Viet Cong wearing black pajamas. One Viet Cong was killed and the area was secured. The First Platoon of A Company flew in and joined up with Blue Team.

The two groups then began a slow and deliberate movement toward the north. The enemy retreated, pausing occasionally to shoot at the advancing units. The helicopter gun ships were able to keep the enemy retreat to a slow pace. They also placed effective fire on any enemy attempt to break out to the sides and get away.

C Company was flown in to block the enemy retreat. They began moving south toward the other units, trapping the enemy. Artillery and air strikes were called into the area. The enemy started breaking into smaller groups and trying to hide. Their attempts to escape proved futile, and the enemy was forced to change their direction to the south straight towards the oncoming Blues and First Platoon. The enemy was now surrounded.

During the operation, a gunship was shot down and the entire crew was killed. First Platoon of C Company located it and stayed there while the rest of C Company continued pushing the stricken enemy.

Once the two friendly elements got close to each other they halted and indirect support from artillery and naval gunfire raked the area between the forces. CH 47 Gun ships, which we affectionately called "Puff the Magic Dragon", strafed the battlefield.

It was now our turn to join the battle. The rest of A Company flew into the area and landed where the downed gunship was still being secured. We moved to the north parallel to C Company. Halts to permit air strikes on the fleeing remains of the Viet Cong soon had us stretched out for a half mile. Lieutenant Denino stayed with the leading elements while I remained towards the rear trying to keep us together.

As we traveled parallel to a small stream the enemy was moving along the other side. With no particular pattern, we would get shot at from across the stream. After we sprayed the opposite bank with every weapon we had, the shooting would stop. We would then move on again.

I had never been that close to an air strike before. The small bombers would streak by thirty to forty feet above the ground. An anchor-shaped object would fall out of the plane in what appeared to be slow motion. When the bomb exploded, it violently shook the ground even on our side of the stream. If we hadn't taken shelter, we would all have been wounded or killed by the flying shrapnel. The plus side was that the small arms fire from across the stream was no longer a concern.

This was a totally different kind of fighting than we were used to. In the Highlands, there was seldom rapid movement by ground forces. Not only did the terrain and vegetation prevent such movement, it wasn't very wise. The enemy could easily have a trap set just waiting for us to barrel in at full steam. Now we had open, flat terrain and an enemy on the run. We also had much more air support. I could get used to this kind of war.

The shoot and run type of fighting was exciting but was beginning to wear some of us down. Gear and ammunition was being discarded frequently. I would have to re-evaluate my equipment needs before our next mission. Another canteen was going to the top of the list. Every time I got near a moving stream to refill my canteen today, I either got shot at or somebody dropped a bomb beside it.

We finally caught up with the lead element. As soon as we arrived, a very excited Mike Riley approached me.

"You should have seen Chuck! He was awesome! He had to take over directing the air strikes. He was talking on two radios at the same time!"

"Where is he?"

Riley paused and motioned to a clump of trees.

"He got hit."

I went over to where Chuck Clendenon was propped against a small tree. The medic was kneeling beside him bandaging a bullet wound to his upper arm.

"I heard you did a great job directing the air strikes. How bad did you get hit?"

"Doc says it's not too bad. I'm probably going home."

We stayed where we were until an evacuation helicopter could come for Clendenon and take him to the hospital. The battle seemed to be over.

All the units relocated to where we had been flown in beside the wrecked helicopter. Blue Team was flown back to LZ Montezuma. C Company returned to LZ Montezuma by foot and assumed our job as Palace Guards. The rest of us got resupplied and settled in for the night. A lone Viet Cong tried to approach our position about nine o'clock that night and was promptly gunned down. The battle was now officially over.

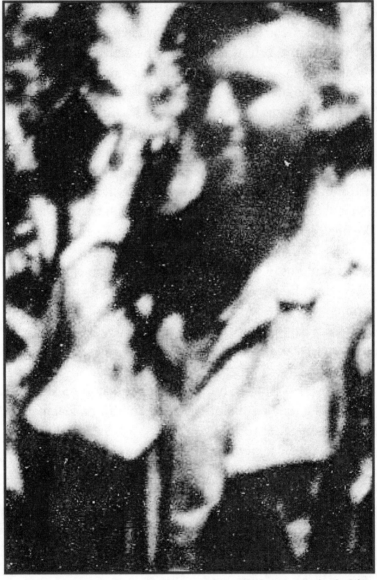

Picture by Permission of Mike Riley

Mike Riley

The four members of the helicopter that got shot down were the only casualties we suffered that day. We counted 42 enemy killed and took two prisoners. Another 11 Viet Cong suspects were captured and detained.

Two days later we learned that Chuck Clendenon had died of his wounds.

LEAVING THE HARD WAY

The day seemed different somehow. A sense of urgency about everything had overcome me. Some unseen force was driving me to do more and be more than ever before. I pondered the cause. Was it just the change in environment from Pleiku and the Highlands to Duc Pho and the Coastal Plain? Or maybe it was being the Sergeant to all these new guys. Maybe it was the difference in missions---guarding roads and bridges as opposed to beating through the jungle in search of the enemy. At least in the jungle we could tell who the enemy was. The only people in the jungle not wearing olive drab were either Montagnard tribesmen---who barely wore any clothing—or North Vietnamese Regular soldiers—who wore uniforms. Here the enemy was very likely the same folks who smiled and waved at you during the day.

The mission for the day seemed very tame—providing security for a civilian crew repairing a section of Highway 1. It took some imagination to call it a highway. It was an unpaved two-lane path. But by Vietnamese standards, it was a major road, important for transportation and supplies. The most curious thing about the mission was that the work crew already had security---a Company of South Vietnamese soldiers. So my best guess was that we were providing security for the security.

Another new group of replacements had arrived that morning. This was beginning to be a daily event. They were lined up looking bewildered and scared at the same time. Some attempted to appear cocky and unconcerned with little success. I came to an abrupt halt in front of one of them. Unbelievable! Sunglasses! The guy is wearing sunglasses! He had no way of knowing that being able to notice just the slightest difference in the shade of a leaf could mean the difference in life or death. One leaf, broken off by a passing enemy and turned so its lighter underside was showing, could give enough warning to change the entire outcome of a battle.

"You've got to get rid of the sunglasses—now!"

"I've got a prescription for them," he stammered as he began to pull a piece of paper out of his shirt pocket.

"Your prescription isn't worth a damn out here."

"Yes, Sergeant."

He reluctantly extracted his issue glasses out of the other shirt pocket and pouted as he placed them on his nose.

Everything seems to be a matter of life or death to me! I really didn't care about anybody's feelings, especially the new guys. Was this the way the old timers felt about me when I first showed up? Probably.

I was no longer taking time to get to know any of the new guys unless they were assigned to my Platoon. In fact, I wasn't getting close to any of them at all. I wasn't even bothering to learn their first names. It was just too painful to get close to someone who may very well be dead tomorrow. I was hard on the new guys—probably harder than I should have been. My bar was set way too high---after all—look who they were supposed to be replacing!

An extra radio had been assigned to us so I assigned a new guy to carry it and be at my side. A sense of urgency was still on me as I directed my Platoon. It really made no sense since we really weren't doing anything. These new guys must have thought I was crazy---and maybe I was.

The ARVN (Army of Republic of Viet Nam) Company had set up a perimeter around the road crew. On both sides of the road a berm rose to a height of between three to four feet, offering a nice protective barrier. We were down the road a small distance patrolling. The day was cooler than usual, and was shaping up to be a very pleasant, uneventful day. Then shots were fired.

We instinctively dove for cover but after several seconds realized we were not the ones under fire. The shooting was coming from the area protected by the ARVNs. I ran to Lt. Denino's side.

"What's going on, Sir?"

"I don't know—not getting any response on the radio."

"I'll go find out."

I was on the way with the radio operator reluctantly on my heels before Lt. Denino nodded his approval. The shooting had stopped by the time I reached the ARVN positions. They were all huddled down as low in the ditches as they could get. None of them even acted like they wanted to look for targets to shoot at.

As I passed two soldiers on my way to the front of the column, one of them pointed at my M-16 and pointed over the berm. I guess since I had an automatic weapon they felt I should take on the enemy by myself. Ignoring this lame request, I moved to where the American advisor was anxiously yelling into his radio.

"Can you reach the damn artillery on your radio? I can't raise a soul. There's a bunker about 200 yards to the right wearing us out! "

I moved to the edge of the burm and peeked over the edge in the direction the advisor had indicated. There it was! It was just a small bump on the otherwise flat landscape. Opening my map with one hand, I reached for the radio handset with the other.

"Fire Mission, over!" I shouted.

I don't know why, but whenever I called for a fire mission, I shouted. I'm sure they couldn't hear me any better.

The radio response from our mortar crew came quickly.

"Fire Mission, out".

Giving the best coordinates I could, I peeked up to see where the first round landed.

The round landed about fifty yards short. As soon as I finished radioing the adjustment, I noticed the strangest thing directly in front of me. It happened so quickly, it was over before I realized what it was. Two inch high eruptions were coming out of the earth in a straight line directly in front of me. One, then a foot closer, another. Another a foot closer and then right in front of me was another.

The next bullet struck me in the left side of my chest with such force it knocked me backwards about three feet. It felt like somebody had kicked me in the ribs. And it burnt like a red-hot rod had been shoved through my body. I rolled over on my back and took a look. A hole about two inches in diameter now occupied the area of my chest where seconds ago my wristwatch had been laced through the top buttonhole of my shirt. The blood bubbled and gurgled every time I took a breath. Sucking chest wound, I remembered from first aid training somewhere.

"Medic!"

I heard myself call for help as I struggled to get the wrapper off my field dressing. The pain had strangely disappeared, but now I had no control over the whole left side of my body.

The advisor for the ARVN unit was suddenly at my side helping me dress my wound.

"Damn, why'd it have to be one of our own guys getting hit! Hang on, I'll call a Dustoff."

After what seemed like an eternity, I could hear the Medivac chopper coming. It hovered above the middle of Highway 1.

The advisor said,"Can you walk?"

"I can't get up, but if you can help me I think I can move."

With one quick movement, he put his shoulder under my left armpit, raising me to my feet. Together, we covered the distance to the waiting chopper, and I felt helping hands raise me up and inside. It seemed my butt no sooner hit the floor than we were lifting up. Then things went black.

When I came to again, a huge black Specialist 5 was hovering over me looking concerned. I recognized him immediately. We had teased him for being a Specialist instead of a Sergeant.

"The difference between you and us is that we can lead troops, and you can't", was the common taunt that usually infuriated him to no end.

We called him "Bird Soldier", since his insignia was an eagle with a stripe under it instead of the three stripes we regular Sergeants wore.

"Hey Bird Soldier," I said weakly.

"I guess I'm going to have to give you NCOs training on applying field dressings," he mumbled as he went about his work.

"What do you mean? I put it on as soon as I got hit!"

"You've got to take it out of the box, stupid!"

After some reflection, I realized he was right. I hadn't taken it out of the box! In my shock and haste I had just placed it over my wound, box and all.

I felt a terrible thirst.

"Give me a drink of water, Bird Soldier!"

"Can't do it. You've got internal injuries. You can't drink anything."

"Please," I begged. "I'm so thirsty."

After a few seconds he took a couple of cotton balls, soaked them in water, and placed them in my mouth.

"That's the best I can do for you. Don't swallow the damn things."

The wet cotton balls were a certain pleasure and relief.

"I'm not stupid enough to swallow a cotton ball!"

"I didn't know. You weren't smart enough to take your field dressing out of the box, so how did I know you wouldn't swallow the cotton balls?"

We both had to grin at that one.

"I gave you a shot. You'll be going to the field hospital by way of LaLa Land."

Then everything got blurry and I was out again.

When I regained consciousness, I had no idea where I was. I was very groggy and had trouble focusing. My glasses were gone. I was in a very big tent of some kind. It was nighttime. I could tell because it was dark except for a small area at the far end of the tent. There was a light on down there where a small group of people gathered around a radio, listening to music and visiting with each other. How I got here I had no idea. All I knew for sure at the moment was that I had a very full bladder.

With a great deal of effort, I managed to get myself upright.

"Gay Boy—what do you think you're doin'?"

I recognized Waycaster's voice immediately. But where was he? It was only then that I saw another bed about six feet away from where I was sitting.

"I've got to take a leak really bad. Where the hell are we, anyway?"

"We're in the Field Hospital. Now lay back down 'fore you hurt yerself!"

"I've really gotta go. Where's the john?"

I struggled trying to swing my legs off the bed.

"Nurse!" shouted Waycaster. "Git yer ass down here! We've got us a real problem!"

Within seconds the bunch from the other end of the tent had swarmed around me. When the light came on I realized why I couldn't go anywhere. I had so many tubes going in and out of my body I looked like a chemistry experiment. Two tubes in my chest, a tube going down my throat, a tube in my arm going up to an IV, and another tube coming out of my penis up to a bag.

"What were you trying to do?" exclaimed the male nurse who seemed to be in charge.

"I had to go."

"You don't have to go anywhere."

He gestured to the suspicious looking tube coming out of my penis.

"You've got a catheter. Go in the bag. Jeez, the Doc would have been really pissed if you'd pulled any tubes loose. Now lie back down and be still!"

We were in the field hospital about a week. I hated the constant changing of dressings because it always hurt. They scrubbed the already sore wounds with gauze pads soaked in surgical soap every time. In addition to the wounds, I had a couple of broken ribs, which made any movement difficult.

Waycaster remained in the bed next to me, although they did pull a curtain between us while changing dressings. He had been The Platoon RTO when he got wounded just a day before me. Standing with his hand stuffed in his pistol belt while he talked on the radio, he had made a tempting target for a sniper. The bullet had entered his buttocks area and exited through the hand and pistol belt.

It was during one of the changing of dressings episodes that he saw his wound for the first time.

"Hey! What the hell have ya'll done to me? Damn, that's not right! That's not right at all!"

The commotion caught the attention of everybody on the ward.

"What is it, Waycaster?" I asked to the curtain.

"These bastards have ruined me! Just ruined me! This isn't right at all. Nosuh, not at all!"

"What happened?"

"They cut out my belly button, that's what!"

The nurse attending him very patiently assured him that he would get along quite well without a belly button.

I didn't laugh. I wanted to, but it hurt my ribs too much.

The next morning Waycaster was gone. He had been moved during the night while I was sleeping. I was so out from the painkillers they were giving me that I never woke up until long after he was gone.

I was soon moved to the general ward. The variety of wounds amazed me. One engineer had been shot with a cleaning rod. He had tried cleaning his rifle while it was loaded. When the rod got stuck he got a buddy to hold the rifle while he pulled on the rod. When the weapon accidentally discharged the rod struck him in the chest. It hurt me just thinking about it. Lots of guys had shrapnel wounds that required a lot of attention. Fortunately, I only required a dressing change two or three times a day.

I really did come to dread something I had to do twice a day. They brought this machine around that I had to blow into. It took a lot of effort to perform this task properly and was very painful since my chest and ribs were very tender. I complained about it until it was explained to me that if I didn't do it I would contract pneumonia and probably lose the use of that lung.

After about a week the two drain tubes in my lung were removed, and I was prepared for transport to the hospital in Okinawa for the rest of my treatment and recovery. Although I could walk with some difficulty, they placed me on a litter and loaded me aboard the plane. We were to stay overnight on Guam and then go on to Okinawa the next day.

It was at Guam that we discovered that I'm allergic to penicillin. The nurse gave me a shot and some other meds and then continued on her rounds. She was responsible for a very large number of wounded soldiers.

I felt myself getting warm at first. That didn't concern me too much—hadn't I been hot for the last nine months? Then it began. My heart started racing—fast then faster. Then it was seemingly out of control, like a car with the accelerator stuck to the floor! It felt as though my heart was going to literally beat out of my chest. I knew that I was surely going to die!

With great difficulty I got somebody's attention. Fortunately, they recognized what was going on and took action. Much more slowly than it had speeded up, my heart beat gradually slowed down to normal.

"Why didn't you tell anybody you were allergic to penicillin?" snapped the nurse.

"I didn't know I was."

"Well, you are. Be sure to tell somebody from now on!"

Believe me, I have. That was one of the most frightening experiences of my life. Any other time, I felt that I could at least do something about the situation, but this time I felt completely helpless and doomed.

The next morning, the human cargo was loaded onto another plane and shipped to the hospital in Okinawa. There I was subjected to daily changes of my dressings accompanied by the scrubbing of my wounds with gauze pads soaked in surgical soap. It was painful at first. The idea was for the wounds to heal from the inside out, rather that scabbing over and leaving pockets to fester. As time went by the wounded area toughened up and the daily scrubbing tickled more than it hurt. It actually felt pretty good, since the wound was beginning to itch.

After a couple weeks of care and physical therapy, I could get around well enough to get a pass to leave the hospital and enjoy the town. Great duty. I didn't have any work assignments, could go to town a few hours every day, and was still drawing combat pay in addition to my regular pay. My brother Fred, who was a Marine stationed at Chu Lai at the time, wrangled a pass, and we spent a few days together in Okinawa. The care I received was outstanding. There were a few glitches, however.

My brother Fred with me in the hospital at Okinawa

When I first got to the hospital, I had no eyeglasses. They had been left behind when I was wounded. It would be weeks before I could get new ones through regular military channels. A letter to my hometown optometrist produced a new pair two weeks before the Army got me a pair. In the meantime, I was my very nearsighted self. Any thing beyond a foot away was a blur.

The head nurse jumped on my case for being so dirty. Nasty dirty is how she put it. I didn't understand what she was talking about. Having gone so long in the field without being able to bathe regularly, I was taking advantage of my newfound luxury and was hitting the showers two and three times a day. I finally asked her to be more specific.

"The bottoms of your feet! Just look at them! They're black they're so dirty!"

I actually couldn't look at them because I couldn't see clearly that far away. Twisting and pulling my foot closer to my face than I would have thought possible, I discovered what she was referring to. The bottoms of my feet were indeed black and dirty, nasty looking. Those months in the jungle walking through the mud and slime had caused dirt to actually be permanently ground into my skin. No amount of scrubbing could remove it. In fact, it would be a year before all the blackness grew out of the bottoms of my feet. Once I explained this to the nurse she dropped the issue, but not before sending an orderly over in one final futile attempt to clean up my nasty feet.

My time in the hospital was finally over. I had gone through physical therapy until my arm and shoulder had regained a full range of motion. The wound on my chest was healed, though still tender. The larger exit wound on my back hadn't completely healed, but it was far enough along that I didn't need to be in the hospital any longer. I needed to treat it daily with cocoa butter to keep the scar tissue from breaking. I would smell like cocoa butter for the next three years.

Lieutenant Putnam had sent me my uniforms and personal belongings. The weapons I had stored in my footlocker weren't forwarded, however. I had stored up quite a nice arsenal of weapons I had picked up here and there. My Bowie knife had gotten lost somewhere along the line. I went through the normal processing procedures and picked up my orders for my next assignment. After a thirty day leave I was to report to Fort Dix, New Jersey to attend Drill Sergeant School.

GOING HOME

I boarded the C-130 cargo plane for the first leg of my trip back home. I was to fly to Alaska, change planes, and then on to Chicago. It was a relief to drop my duffle bag to the ground as my eyes got accustomed to the darkness of the cargo hold. I had been carrying the bag on my good shoulder but I was still weak.

My vision returned to me slowly. I surveyed the other passengers on the plane. Caskets! There had to be twenty of them. I was just standing there staring when the airman in charge came up and stood beside me.

"Hope you don't mind, Sarge. You can always get off and wait until tomorrow for another flight."

"No, no, it's okay," I stammered, my eyes still fixed on the coffins.

"Well, grab a seat and get comfortable. We're about to take off."

There were no real seats, just a wide strip of cargo netting running the length of the cargo hold on either side. I stumbled over to the left side of the plane and fell into the netting. The roar of the engines insured that there would be no further conversations with the airman.

The trip gave me time to reflect. Looking at the stack of caskets, I couldn't help but wonder who was inside them. Was it another Guimonde or Chace? Castelda, Garner, Karopczc, Miranda, Perez, Perone, Rhoads, Rugerro, Chamberlain, Mercato-Santos, Clendenon, or any of the other men from A Company who would come home in this fashion? Were they veteran NCOs or nineteen year old kids who just months ago were innocently living good lives, circled by loving friends and family? Were they guys just like me who just weren't as lucky?

I was really having a very hard time keeping faith in any kind of God. What kind of loving God would allow this to happen? Why did so many young men have to die before they had a chance to even live? Why did those of us who made it through it all have to return to a society that hated us personally for doing what we were raised to believe was the right and honorable thing to do?

I was thankful to be alone. Tears streamed down my face as I sat in the darkness of the cabin pondering these and many other questions. It was really the first time I had been able to have the time and opportunity to mourn my fallen comrades. The events of my tour had been so intense and happened so quickly that there had been no time to actually think about them. Thinking about them now in the presence of those not as fortunate as I was made me extremely sad and angry at the same time.

Some time during the flight I must have fallen asleep. When the plane touched down on the frozen airstrip in Alaska I was jarred back to reality. We finally came to a halt in front of the terminal. I picked up my bag and stepped out, leaving the other passengers behind.

The frigid Alaska air blew through my jungle fatigues as if they didn't exist. My mind went immediately to when I first stepped off the plane in Viet Nam. The heat then overwhelmed me as much as the cold was affecting me now. I got inside as quickly as possible.

Five cups of coffee and two hours later I was on a civilian flight to Chicago O'Hare Airport. The contrast between this flight and the Spartan military plane was incredible. Even though I was flying coach class, I felt like royalty. Comfortable seats, snacks and drinks, pretty, friendly stewardesses----it just doesn't get any better than this, I told myself.

When I got to O'Hare' I picked up my bag and went outside to find a taxi to take me to the train station. I was totally unprepared for what happened next. Just outside the door, a group of war protesters swarmed me.

As a kid I heard my father and uncles tell me what a glorious time it was when they returned from overseas. Crowds of people had surrounded them, cheering and thanking them for their service. . This crowd wasn't cheering, they were jeering. They surrounded me, shouting obscenities. They were calling me a baby killer. One girl came up and spat on me. The more I tried to protest the more vocal they got.

Just when I had taken all I was going to, a Yellow Cab drove through the crowd honking his horn.

"Get In!" he commanded.

He didn't have to tell me twice.

"Damned Hippies!" he declared." I just want you to know we all don't feel that way. Welcome home, Son!"

As he drove me to the train station I sat in silence as he carried on about how disrespectful the demonstrators had been. I was still stunned. I couldn't believe what had just happened. I had never killed any babies! The only people I had killed were trying to kill me!

I tried to pay the cabbie when he dropped me off at the train station but he wouldn't accept any money. He pointed to my Combat Infantry Badge. "You've paid enough!"

The train station in Chicago was a very interesting and busy place. It would have been alright with me to sit there all day just to watch the people go by. I do believe that if I had just sat there long enough I would have truly seen everything. After an hour of people watching, I boarded the train for Bloomington.

I had called my sister before I left Chicago. Merry was five years older than me and more like a mother than a sister. When I stepped off the train she was the first person I saw. My niece and nephew, Dana and Ricky, were with her. After a lot of hugging, accompanied by the appropriate amount of tears, we loaded my bag in the trunk of her car and headed home.

Home. What a wonderful word. There had been more than one time I was convinced I would never come home again. I was certain that my next homecoming would be posthumously. But here I was.

We drove for an hour across the flat Central Illinois countryside. There were no jungles or mountains. No rice paddies, just corn and soybeans as far as you could see. And I could see for miles! Yes, it was great to be home again.

We got to the house and went in. Not only were my mother and two younger sisters there, but my father was home too. He was never home during the day. The most amazing thing was that he was sober. I tried to remember the last time I had seen him sober. I couldn't.

We spent several minutes hugging and celebrating our reunion. When there was a pause in the conversation, Dad stood in front of me.

"Let me see the medal."

The request took me by complete surprise. I went to my duffle bag and dug through until my hand touched the case that contained my Purple Heart. He took it, opened it, and just stood there staring at it. Then without a word, he did something I had never seen my father do. He went into the bedroom, put the medal on the bed, and dropped to his knees in prayer.

"You have no idea what it did to him when he heard you were in Okinawa. That's where he was in the War, you know." My mother said in a hushed tone as we stood watching in awe.

I did remember. He had told me about his experience at the battle for Okinawa during World War II. He and his fellow crew members had stood on the deck of their troop transport, the USS Anne Arundel, and watched the battle rage back and forth until it was finally over. Enemy planes flew over them, strafing the decks and even crashing, Kamikaze style, into the ship next to them. The enemy floated a barge loaded with explosives towards them which they had to blow up, crew and all. After the battle, he was in the party that went ashore and recovered the wounded. The whole experience had scarred him so deeply that he only talked about it when drinking, always with a tear in his eye.

After a nice dinner and lots of lively conversation, my sister Merry and her kids loaded up and went home. My younger sisters, Marti and Gretchen, tackled their homework before going to bed. Mom settled in front of the television with her knitting. Dad and I sat on the front porch. As usual, the conversation was very thin. After an hour, I went into the house and slept in my own bed for the first time in a year. All the lumps were right where I had left them.

I don't know what woke me up. It took me some time to figure out where I actually was. I had clean sheets instead of a dingy poncho liner. My feet were bare. Instinctively, I felt around for my rifle. When I finally realized where I was, I beamed from ear to ear like a child at Christmas. Easing myself out of bed, I wandered to the kitchen. I didn't bother looking for a coffee pot. I don't remember my parents ever having one. Instead I heated some water and loaded a cup with the instant coffee that was always on the counter.

It was still a little before sunrise and nobody else was stirring. Coffee cup in hand, I eased the screen door open and stepped out onto the porch. It was almost cool, even though it was July. A gentle breeze was blowing, but of course there was always a breeze here. I settled into the old rocking chair and lit my first cigarette of the day.

Silently, gloriously, the sun began to rise. How amazing it was to actually see the sun clear the horizon. I could feel the heat begin to warm my body almost as soon as the sun was fully visible. The birds began their chorus, slowly at first. The volume quickly increased with every chirp that joined in. It was almost as if they were saying "Welcome home, Curt!"-----Welcome Home..

HONORS

A COMPANY 2/35TH INFANTRY REGIMENT

The Congressional Medal of Honor is the highest military decoration awarded by the United States of America. It is received by members of our military who distinguish themselves "conspicuously by gallantry and intrepidity at the risk of his or her life above and beyond the call of duty while engaged in an action against an enemy of the United States. During the ten year duration of the Viet Nam war, the Medal of Honor was only awarded to 246 individuals. Two of these were members of A Company. Lieutenant Stephen E. Karopczyc received his posthumously for his actions March 12, 1967.

The second highest award for valor is the Distinguished Service Cross. Five members of A Company received this award, including Specialist Four Wendell T. Meade and Staff Sergeant James H. Hill, Jr.

We earned the Valorous Unit Award, Meritorious Unit Citation, Republic of Viet Nam Cross of Gallantry with Palm, and the Republic of Viet Nam Civil Action Honor Medal, First Class.

Many of us earned the Silver Star and Bronze Star for Valor, which are the third and fourth highest awards for bravery in action. Most of us were awarded the Purple Heart for the physical wounds we suffered. All of us earned the Combat Infantryman Badge.

None of us returned as the same person we were when we arrived in Viet Nam.

GLOSSARY

Ak-47- A Soviet or Chinese manufactured assault rifle. It could fire automatic or semi-automatic. It gave the enemy a lot of firepower since it could fire rapidly and was highly portable.

Area of Operation-The section of country assigned a unit to operate in. Sometimes another unit would be operating in an adjoining area so it was important not to stray and get shot by mistake.

Combat Infantryman Badge (CIB)- A permanent award given to soldiers who have actually been in combat with the enemy. A silver flintlock rifle is displayed on a blue background with a silver wreath around it. Since it is only awarded to infantry, it is a highly prized and rare decoration.

Command Post-When a unit sets up a defensive position it is usually a circle or an oblong. Whoever is the main leader will set up an impromptu headqu.arters where he can easily direct operations. This is generally in the center of the formation. The Commander, his radio operator, Forward Observer, and the Medic are the foundation of this group, but it could include others.

Company—A Company consisted of three platoons and a command group. A Captain led the company assisted by two radio operators, a First Sergeant, a medic, and often a Forward Observer from the artillery. The Forward Observer directed the artillery and air support.

C-rations-Canned food rations provided for combat situations. The meals can allegedly be eaten hot or cold. Suitable if you have absolutely nothing else to eat.

C-4- A moldable plastic explosive. Often wrapped around trees to clear an area for landing helicopters. Burns rapidly with intense heat. A marble sized piece would heat coffee or C-rations in seconds.

Door Gunner- These guys sat in the doors of helicopters with a machine gun mounted in front of them. This was the only armament most helicopters had. Unsung heroes of the war, they sat exposed to enemy fire and often provided support for the infantry as the troops loaded and unloaded.

Forward Observer (FO)-An Artillery officer assigned to an infantry company to direct artillery and air support for the unit

Grunt-Slang expression for an infantryman. Since they carried everything they might need on their backs, a soldier in the field would be carrying around 60 pounds in extreme heat through a jungle. Since there would be a lot of grunting going on, Grunt became their unofficial nickname.

Gunship- A heavily armed helicopter equipped for close support. Rocket launchers. grenade launchers, and rapid fire machine guns were typical armament for these helicopters. Since they could maneuver in close contact with the enemy, they were very effective.

Ho Chi Minh Trail-Heavily traveled supply route from North Viet Nam to the south. Since most of it went through Cambodia and Laos, the enemy could freely move troops and supplies to staging areas just across the border. During my time in Viet Nam, we were not allowed to cross these borders and attack. The trail was bombed almost daily but the enemy had enough troops in place to repair the damage almost immediately.

Killed In Action (KIA)- Term used to denote a soldier killed as a direct result of combat.

Landing Zone (LZ)- A designated area for helicopters to take off and land. An area free of trees and other obstructions was necessary for helicopters to take off and land. Even though they could land almost vertically, such a movement exposed them to enemy fire. Once loaded, a helicopter needs horizontal as well as vertical movement to gain altitude.

Listening Post (LP)- Two or three men positioned a short ways in front of the main defensive position, usually at night. They usually had a radio with them and were out there to warn the main body in case of approaching enemy activity.

M-16 Rifle- The standard weapon carried by most American troops in Viet Nam. It had a selector switch to allow for automatic or semi-automatic firing. It fired the 5.56 mm round common to all NATO troops.

M-60 Machine Gun- Each Platoon had at least one M-60. It was designed to fire belts of ammunition continuously. The bullets were a larger round than the M-16 (7.62 mm) and added much more firepower.

M-79 Grenade Launcher- A shoulder fired weapon to launch 40mm grenade rounds at the enemy. Not as effective as artillery or mortars, but instantly available since at least one was always carried by a platoon member.

NCO-Non-Commissioned Officer-Designation of an enlisted man, usually a Sergeant, in a leadership position

North Vietnamese Army (NVA)- Soldiers trained and equipped in North Vietnam and sent down to South Viet Nam to fight. These troops should not be confused with the guerilla soldiers of the Viet

Cong. North Vietnamese regulars wore uniforms, were well equipped and trained, and would be found with units of battalion size. Most of the enemies found in the Central Highlands were NVA and very formidable opponents.

Platoon—A platoon consisted of three squads and were commanded by a Lieutenant. Two machine gun teams were assigned to a platoon and either worked with a squad or teamed up to form a heavy weapons squad. A radio operator, Platoon Sergeant, and a medic were normally part of the the Platoon command team with the Lieutenant.

Radio Telephone Operator (RTO)- A soldier assigned to carry the radio for the commander of the unit. Usually there was at least one RTO per platoon and two others with the Company commander. With the radio and spare battery in addition to his regular combat gear, the RTO would be packing 100 pounds of equipment. He also was a prime target, since the radio was the lifeline of the unit, allowing communication with air and artillery support.

Saddle Up-Put on your equipment and prepare to move out.

Search-and-Destroy Mission- A large force, usually of Company size, would be sent into an area of suspected enemy activity. The mission was to search for the enemy and destroy them and any equipment or supplies they may have stockpiled in the area. We conducted a great many of these missions, usually only finding where the enemy had been. A lot of camps and rice were destroyed.

Squad—The smallest unit in an infantry company referred to in this book. Our squad consisted of four to ten members and was usually led by a Sergeant. There were three squads in our platoon.

Squelch- The raspy noise of static that constantly came from our radios when they were on and not in use. The noise would stop when the button on the side of the hand-held microphone was depressed. Everybody close to the radio would pay attention when the squelch stopped, indicating that a message was coming. "Keying the mike", which meant pushing the button to speak, was often used when it was dangerous to speak but communication was essential. As an example, a listening post or ambush position had to remain silent. At a predetermined time, the outpost would "key the mike", thus "breaking the squelch". One break usually meant "Yes" or "everything is okay" and two breaks meant "No" or "Send help- we're in trouble out here!"

INFANTRY UNITS

Unit	Soldiers	Leader
Squad	8-13	Squad leader---Sergeant
Platoon	26-55	Platoon Leader---Lieutenant
Company	80-225	Company Commander---Captain
Battalion	300-1,300	Battalion Commander-Lieutenant Colonel
Regiment	1,000–3,000	Regimental Commander--Colonel
Brigade	3,000–5,000	Brigade Commander-Brigadier General
Division	10,000–15,000	Division Commander-Major General

ARMY RANKS

Enlisted Rank

E-1	E-2	E-3	E-4	E-4
No Insignia				
Private	Private	Private First Class	Specialist	Corporal

E-5	E-6	E-7	E-8	E-8
Sergeant	Staff Sergeant	Sergeant First Class	Master Sergeant	First Sergeant

Sergeant Major	Command Sergeant Major	Sergeant Major of the Army

Officers

O-1	O-2	O-3	O-4	O-5
Second Lieutenant	First Lieutenant	Captain	Major	Lieutenant Colonel

O-6	O-7	O-8	O-9	O-10
Colonel	Brigadier General	Major General	Lieutenant General	General

Need A Fundraiser?

Sell this Book

Special pricing available to
Clubs and Organizations

Contact us for Details
CPG Publishing Company
P. O. Box 73161
Durham, NC 27712-3161
cpgpub@yahoo.com

LaVergne, TN USA
29 March 2011
221924LV00003B/3/P